D1085203

HUMAN LEARNING

HUMAN LEARNING

EDWARD L. THORNDIKE

THE M.I.T. PRESS
MASSACHUSETTS INSTITUTE OF TECHNOLOGY
CAMBRIDGE, MASSACHUSETTS, AND LONDON, ENGLAND

First printing 1931 by
The Century Company

First M.I.T. Press Paperback Edition, March, 1966

MANUFACTURED IN THE UNITED STATES OF AMERICA

PREFACE

Parts of this book present facts and principles which I have presented more fully and technically elsewhere. This is especially true of Lectures 9, 10, and 11, which abound in restatement or quotation. Other facts, including the bulk of Lectures 1 to 6, present facts and principles which are outcomes of investigations of the years 1927 to 1930, made possible by a grant from the Carnegie Corporation. A full technical account of these will be published elsewhere. The treatment here is necessarily superficial, but not, I think, misleading. I am encouraged by the comments of those who heard the lectures to hope that those who may read them will find them a useful account of fundamental facts and principles of human learning.

E. L. T.

January, 1931

CONTENTS

HUMAN LEARNING

Lecture 1

INTRODUCTION: THE INFLUENCE OF THE FREQUENCY OF OCCURRENCE OF A SITUATION

IT has seemed that the best service which I can perform for the university and the donor of the Messenger lectureship is to present to you certain facts and theories concerning the nature and evolution of human learning. This subject is intrinsically of great interest. Man's power to change himself, that is, to learn, is perhaps the most impressive thing about him. Modern theories explaining it will help acquaint us with certain important theories of the mind as a whole. This topic is closely and emphatically relevant to the problem of the Evolution of Civilization, specified in the donor's gift. Civilization is, indeed, the chief product of human learning. Homes and tools, language and art, customs and laws, science and religion are all created by changes in the minds of men. Their maintenance and use also depend on human modifiability—the ability of man to learn. If that were reduced by half, in the sense that the next generation could learn only things half as hard to learn as those which man now can learn, most of human civilization would be unusable by the next generation and would soon vanish off the face of the earth. For example, most, if not all, that is taught in this university nobody could then learn. The contents of drug stores would poison us. Ships and trains and automobiles, if they moved at all, would go in somewhat the disorder of the toy boats and trains of children.

3

Human learning consists of changes in the nature and behavior of human beings. Changes in nature are known to us only by changes in behavior. The word *behavior* as used here and later means anything which the human animal does. It includes thoughts and feelings as truly as movements, and makes no assumptions concerning the deeper nature of any of these. It takes them as they are found.

It is convenient to express a man's life in terms of the situations or states of affairs which he encounters, the reactions or responses which he makes to them, and the connections whereby the millions of situations lead to or evoke the responses which they do. The situations and responses of a human life are obviously not haphazard. If a certain situation, call it S_1, occurs in a certain man's life, he is not equally likely to make any one of the million, or more, responses which a man can make. On the contrary, S_1 usually has well-marked tendencies to call forth some one particular response or some one of certain few responses. The term connections is used to express these tendencies for a given situation to evoke certain responses rather than others. For S_1 to connect with R_{27} means that S_1 tends to evoke or be followed by R_{27} more often than a mere haphazard arrangement of situations and responses would allow.

As a man lives and learns, his reaction or response to the same situation or state of affairs changes. Whereas once the question "What is the cube root of sixty-four?" evoked the response of silent indifference or "I don't know" or "What does that mean?" it later evokes a prompt response of "Four." We say that a connection has been formed between *cube root of sixty-four* and *four*.

Such a connection may exist in various degrees of strength. The connection between "Write the word *repeat*" and writing the six letters *r-e-p-e-a-t* in that order may be so strong that the man can always write it even if half asleep, or it may be only strong enough to operate in nine cases out of ten when he is awake and alert; or it may be so weak that it will operate less often than *r-e-p-e-t-e* or *r-e-p-p-e-e-t*.

The strength of a connection between any given situation such as S_1, and any given response, such as R_{27}, means the degree of probability that S_1 will be followed by R_{27}. Thus if S_1 is the thought, "How much is nine times seven?" and R_{27} is the thought, "Sixty-three," the connection in a person well trained in arithmetic is very strong. If that situation recurs 1,000 times, it will be followed by that response probably in 990 of them. Only very rarely will some other response occur. The strength of $S_1 \rightarrow R_{27}$ is approximately .990 for that individual. If the same situation occurred in a child just beginning to learn the facts about multiplication by nine and by seven, that connection would be much weaker. It might have a probability of occurrence of only one in four or .250.

Learning consists, in part, of changes in the strength of $S \rightarrow R$ connections, such as this increase from .250 to .990 for $S_1 \rightarrow R_{27}$.

Learning consists also in just having new responses. A person changes who adds to his repertory of say 963,728 responses ten new ones R_{963729} to R_{963738}. These new responses come, however, always in connection with something. For one of them to come into being means that some situation connects with them, and so, as we shall later see, changes the probabilities of response to that situation. So it is a matter of convenience whether we think of learning as acquiring responses and changing the strength of their connections with the situations of life, or as the latter alone. The same holds true of learning by getting rid of certain responses, losing them from one's repertory. Getting entirely rid of a response is the reduction of all the connections leading from all situations to it to zero strength.

We may think of any situation as having some infinitesimal probability of evoking from a given individual any response out of an enormous number, even conceivably out of all the responses of which that individual is capable. "How much is nine times seven?" may conceivably make a person think, not of "sixty-three," but of "Shakspere" or "a bottle of ink" or of "seventy times seven." When we say that a certain connection has zero strength, we usually do not distinguish between truly zero strength and such infinitesimal probabilities as one in 10,000,000; often there is no need to.

Learning is, however, real—even though it changes the probability of a connection only to one in 10,000, if the previous probability was less than that. Moreover, these very low degrees of strength are sometimes of enormous importance. Let us suppose, for example, that a certain connection, $S_{693} \rightarrow R_{7281}$ has a strength of one in 10,000 in each of 1,000,000 men. Then, if S_{693} occurs once today to each of these men, 100 men will probably respond with R_{7281}. The difference between 100 doing so and none doing so might cause a score of murders or a war or a great invention or some outstanding act of philanthropy. Also, the learning to a strength of .99 or 1.00 from a strength of .0001 may be far easier than from a strength of .0000. In the former case the response at least exists as a possibility.

Connections of 1.00 Strength

Connections which seem perfectly sure to operate may really be of different strengths. They may all have strengths of 1.00 for the person under ordinary circumstances and at the present date, but one of them may be so strong that an enormous amount of excitement or distraction or lapse of time without practice would not prevent the person from surely making the response in question to the situation in question; whereas another of them may be insecure if the person becomes excited or sleepy or goes a year without practice. Much of learning consists in adding strength to connections so that they will resist disturbing conditions or the destructive effect of disuse.

When the strength of a connection is increased from zero or an infinitesimal, we usually speak of *forming the connection.* When it is increased from some substantial strength to greater strength, we usually speak of *strengthening the connection.* There is no fundamental difference.

The word *connection* has been used without prejudice concerning what physiological event or condition parallels or constitutes it. It is, so far, simply an expression of the probability that a certain S will be followed by a certain R. *Bond,* or *link,* or *relation,* or *tendency,* or any still more colorless word, may be put in its place.

Learning may comprise not only changes in the strength of connections between situations and responses, and the acquisition of new responses, but also changed sensitivity or attentiveness to situations and parts of situations. The general dynamics of those changes will be found to be the same as for connection-forming, and no more need be said about them.

The account of learning which I have so far given is intentionally naïve and superficial. It may easily be criticized as follows: First, How much of the total state of affairs outside a man is included in the situation? "What is the cube root of sixty-four?" or "How much is nine times seven?" is surely only a tiny fragment of what the person was influenced by at the time. Second, How much of the total behavior of the man at the time is the response? He looked and breathed and did many other things besides say "I don't know" or "Four." Third, The actual total situations and responses being thus usually very complicated affairs, how do we know which part of an *S* evokes any given part of an *R*? Fourth, Where does the situation leave off and its response begin?

These and other more subtle questions and objections and qualifications are reasonable, and in due time we may consider them, but it is not, I think, profitable for us to do so now. *Situation, response, connection,* and *strength of connection* are a naïve and superficial, but very convenient, vocabulary to aid me in presenting certain facts about learning. These facts will be true and valuable regardless of the vocabulary in which they are presented. Let me then postpone a rigorous treatment of the terms we use until we need it for understanding the facts themselves.

The facts to which we may turn first were obtained in an investigation of these questions: What happens when a man is confronted again and again by the same situation? What would happen if a man could be subjected to the same situation say 1,000 times, with everything else in the world and in him kept constant save the thousand repetitions of the situation and the changes, if any, which they produce in him? We are, that is, seeking to determine the influence of the mere repetition of a situation, all else being equal.

Consider, for example, the following experiment: You sit at your desk with a large pad of paper and a pencil, close your eyes, say, "Draw a four-inch line with one quick movement," and again and again draw with one quick shove a line intended to be four inches long. You keep your eyes closed throughout. Day after day you do this until you have drawn 3,000 lines, no one of which you have ever seen. You have then responded to approximately the same situation— "Draw a four-inch line with one quick shove of the same pencil on the same pad in the same position"—3,000 times.

TABLE I

DISTRIBUTION OF THE RESPONSES AT EACH SITTING IN DRAWING LINES TO EQUAL 4″ WITH
EYES CLOSED: SUBJECT T

Frequencies in Sittings 1 to 12

Response	1	2	3	4	5	6	7	8	9	10	11	12
3.7									1			
3.8								2				
3.9												
4.0			3						3			
4.1			4	1				1	3			2
4.2		4	8			1		3	6	1	2	1
4.3		3	9	1				4	5	3		4
4.4		13	12	6			3	4	12	2	4	3
4.5	3	18	18	14	2	7	3	15	14	8	7	11
4.6		20	23	23	3	7	8	13	14	8	14	11
4.7	6	20	14	22	11	14	16	25	13	9	14	21
4.8	6	22	15	18	14	27	17	16	18	15	19	26
4.9	13	17	24	24	22	28	18	21	16	10	18	30
5.0	25	20	16	24	26	21	29	25	14	24	19	20
5.1	27	10	16	12	25	32	14	15	14	22	31	22
5.2	24	11	8	12	24	21	23	25	16	18	28	16
5.3	30	8	2	11	21	13	17	8	18	18	16	12
5.4	17	4	2	8	10	10	7	8	12	12	7	7
5.5	12	1		4	13	8	7	3	10	13	4	3
5.6	7			2	4	7	4	1	4	5	2	2
5.7	3			1	4	2	5	2	6		3	1
5.8				1				1	2			
5.9	1			1					1		2	
6.0												
6.1									1			
6.2	1						1					
Total	175	171	174	183	181	198	172	192	200	175	190	192
Median	5.23	4.83	4.77	4.93	5.15	5.07	5.07	4.96	4.97	5.13	5.09	4.96
Q *	.16	.22	.23	.22	.19	.19	.21	.24	.33	.24	.21	.20

* *Q* is the half of the range required to include the middle 50 per cent of the responses.

Table 1 shows the results of such an experiment. It illustrates two general truths or principles: (1) that of multiple response or variable reaction, and (2) that of the failure of repetition of the situation to cause learning.

The response varies in the first sitting from 4.5 inches to 6.2 inches; in the second, from 4.2 inches to 5.5 inches; in the third, from 4.0 inches to 5.4 inches; and similarly in the others. For the whole experiment it varies from 3.7 inches to 6.2 inches. Such a multiplicity of response to a situation that is as nearly the same as we can make it, by an individual in as nearly the same condition as we can keep him, is the rule. In another experiment a subject was repeatedly submitted to the situation, "Spell the long *e* sound" as an incident in the task of spelling a long series of three-syllable nonsense words pronounced by the experimenter, such as *kace-eed'aub, weece'-ol-eet, kawl-awt-eez'.* He will write sometimes *e*, sometimes *ee,* sometimes *ie,* sometimes *ei,* sometimes *i.* There are subtle differences in the brain and nerves and muscles of the individual from minute to minute which cause a multiplicity or variety of responses to the same external situation.

Repetition of the situation 3,000 times caused no learning. The lines drawn in the eleventh and twelfth sittings are not demonstrably better than or different from those drawn in the first and second. Table 2 represents the results of the experiment taken backward, but if you did not know this and had been asked to choose the one which represented the course of learning, you would have chosen one as often as the other. And so would any group of psychological experts.

It has been supposed by many in the past that the mere repetition of a situation, in and of itself, somehow causes learning. The "how" has often been left as a mystery, but in one theory of excellent origin and repute, it has been ex-

TABLE 2

DISTRIBUTION OF RESPONSES IN TABLE 1 TAKEN BACKWARD

Frequencies in Sittings 1 to 12

Response	1	2	3	4	5	6	7	8	9	10	11	12
3.7				1								
3.8				2								
3.9												
4.0				3					3			
4.1	2			3	1				1	4		
4.2	1	2	1	6	3		1			8	4	
4.3	4		3	5	4				1	9	3	
4.4	3	4	2	12	4	3			6	12	13	
4.5	11	7	8	14	15	3	7	2	14	18	18	3
4.6	11	14	8	14	13	8	7	3	23	23	20	
4.7	21	14	9	13	25	16	14	11	22	14	20	6
4.8	26	19	15	18	16	17	27	14	18	15	22	6
4.9	30	18	10	16	21	18	28	22	24	24	17	13
5.0	20	19	24	14	25	29	21	26	24	16	20	25
5.1	22	31	22	14	15	14	32	25	12	16	10	27
5.2	16	28	18	16	25	23	21	24	12	8	11	24
5.3	12	16	18	18	8	17	13	21	11	2	8	30
5.4	7	7	12	12	8	7	10	10	8	2	4	17
5.5	3	4	13	10	8	7	8	13	4		1	12
5.6	2	2	5	4	1	4	7	4	2			7
5.7	1	3	4	6	2	5	2	4	1			3
5.8			2		1			1				
5.9		2	1					1				1
6.0												
6.1			1									
6.2					1							1
Total	192	190	175	200	192	172	198	181	183	174	171	175
Median	4.96	5.09	5.13	4.97	4.96	5.07	5.07	5.15	4.93	4.77	4.83	5.23
Q	.20	.21	.24	.33	.24	.21	.19	.19	.22	.23	.22	.16

plained as the result of a tendency of the more frequent connection to subtract strength from those less frequent, to increase its strength by a sort of drainage into it from them. In our experiment, according to this theory, the connections from the situation, "Draw a four-inch line" to the responses producing lengths of 5.0, 5.1, 5.2, and 5.3, which had a frequency of 106 (as against 69 for all the others) in the first sitting, should gain in the next and later sittings.

Nothing of the sort occurred in the experiment. The responses 5.0, 5.1, 5.2, and 5.3 do not wax at the expense of 4.5 or 5.7. Nothing of the sort occurred in the experiment in spelling the long *e* sound and other sounds. For example, consider these figures for the sound of hissing *s*. The response of spelling it by a single *s* was enormously more frequent than any other response such as *c* or *ss,* occurring more than twelve times as often as all others put together at the beginning of our experiment. Yet it did not increase its frequency as the situation was repeated again and again. So also, with single *o* for the long *o* sound, and single *a* for the sound of *a* as in *make* or *late*. Each is enormously more frequent than any other for its situation, yet the connection leading to it does not drain away strength from the connections leading to other responses. At the beginning of the experiment, the three show a strength of 4 to 1 for all others combined; and at the end of the experiment, a strength of 4 to 1.*

It will be understood, of course, that repetition of a situation is ordinarily followed by learning, because ordinarily we reward certain of the connections leading from it and punish others by calling the responses to which they respectively lead right or wrong, or by otherwise favoring and thwarting them. Had I opened my eyes after each shove of the pencil during the second and later sittings,

* 2,094 to 516 and 2,080 to 530.

and measured the lines and been desirous of accuracy in the task, the connections leading to 3.8, 3.9, 4.0, 4.1, and 4.2 would have become more frequent until I reached my limit of skill in the task. If the experiment had been in learning to spell the words and if the subjects had been told after each response whether it was right or wrong, the connections leading to the right responses, whether frequent or rare at the start, would have waxed. Our question is whether the mere repetition of a situation in and of itself causes learning, and in particular whether the more frequent connections tend, just because they are more frequent, to wax in strength at the expense of the less frequent. Our answer is *No.*

This question is so fundamental that I have sought to check our negative answer by increasing the number of subjects and by using a wide variety of experiments in which connections of great frequency are given opportunity to drain off strength from those of less frequency. I will report one in which the initial frequency is given such an opportunity, and the satisfyingness and annoyingness of the consequences are also given a certain opportunity to act. A very long list of beginnings of words (*ab, ac, ad, af, ba, be, bi, bo,* and the like) is prepared, and individuals are requested to add to each of them one or more letters to make a word. They do 240 such completions each day for fourteen days. Certain of these beginnings of words occurred twenty-eight times in the course of the experiment, so that we have for each individual with each situation a record like that shown in Table 3 for Individual C with *el.*

In this case there is learning. Subject C has clearly changed in the direction of writing *f* to complete *el* into *elf,* but not by an increase of the initially frequent and decrease of the initially rare. There is an increase of short completions and a decrease of long completions. Writing *f*

is easier than writing *evate* or *ephant,* and it is quicker.*
C's record with *el* is typical. One-letter responses gain, no
matter how infrequent they were in the beginning. When
the number of letters used is constant there is no greater
gain for the initially more frequent.

TABLE 3

RESPONSES OF INDIVIDUAL C IN COMPLETING *el*

First 8		*Last 8*
evate		f
ephant	(Twelve inter-	f
ephant	mediate re-	f
evate	sponses not	f
ephant	reported here.)	f
ephant		f
ephant		f
f		f

The details of the other experiments we need not discuss. Their general result is in agreement with the samples
so far described. So far as I can now see, the repetition of
a situation in and of itself has no selective power. If a certain state of affairs acts upon a man 10,000 times, he will,
so far as any intrinsic action of the 10,000 repetitions is
concerned, respond in the same way to the last thousand as
to the first. The repetition of a situation may change a man
as little as the repetition of a message over a wire changes
the wire. In and of itself, it may teach him as little as the
message teaches the switchboard. In particular, the more
frequent connections are not selected by their greater frequency.

Two consequences of these findings may be noted briefly.
All psychological theories of inhibition by drainage are made

* The subjects of the experiment were not urged to speed, but the
time of completing the 240 words was recorded and it would naturally
be a matter of some pride to lower it.

more dubious than ever, since our experiments showed negative results for very favored cases of such drainage. All educational doctrines which attach value to experience or activity as such, irrespective of the direction of the experience or activity and of its consequences, are made less acceptable than before. Experience, in the sense of merely confronting and responding to the situations of life, can hardly be a powerful agent for either good or harm when several thousand repetitions of such an experience do so little.

Lecture 2

THE INFLUENCE OF THE FREQUENCY OF OCCURRENCE OF A CONNECTION: THE PRINCIPLE OF BELONGING

IN the previous lecture we investigated the changes produced in a mind by its repeated subjection to the same situation. To-day we shall investigate the changes produced in a mind by its repeated operating of the same connection.

In the ordinary experiments upon learning the individual knows what he is to learn. He is consequently satisfied by what makes, or seems to make, progress toward it. It is then difficult to obtain any measurements of the potency of repetition alone. In memorizing lists of pairs, for example, the subject is better satisfied when he holds the material in mind for a second or so after hearing or seeing it than when he loses it. If, on hearing the first member of a pair, he anticipates the second member, he is notably satisfied when his anticipatory reaction is correct. So "number of repetitions" in the ordinary experiments means in part also "number of opportunities for satisfying or annoying after-effects to operate."

We have sought to obtain closer approximations to the activity of repetition without the influence of the consequences of the connection, by using a different form of presentation of the connected pairs, by instructing the subjects in certain ways and by concealing or disguising the learning which we later test.

The most usual plan of our experiments to this end is to

present long series of pairs (from about 500 to 4,000) in which certain pairs recur often, with instructions to the subject to listen comfortably without any effort to remember and without thinking about what is heard, just experiencing what is provided. A second plan is to have the subjects of the experiment copy the pairs or write them from dictation, the experiment being described as a means of obtaining data on fatigue, or on speed and accuracy, or on lapses.

Suppose, for example, that I read to you this series of names and numbers and you write the number connected with each name as I read it: Amogio 29, Barona 72, Delose 68, Barona 72, Delfonso 18, Palesand 51, Amogio 29, Nanger 79, Raskin 60, Geno 15, Barona 72, Palesand 51, until I have read a long series containing ninety different names each followed by a different number from 10 to 99, with Amogio 29, Barona 72, and certain other pairs occurring 100 times each; with Delose 68, Delfonso 18, and certain other pairs occurring fifty times each; with Palesand 51, Nanger 79, and other pairs occurring twenty-five times each; and so on down to pairs that occur only six or three times.

The connection between hearing a certain name and writing a certain number will then have been repeated a certain number of times in you. If, at the end of such an experiment, you hear the names and write down after each the first two-figure number that comes to mind, the numbers which you write will depend in part upon these repetitions of the connections. You will think of *29* after hearing Amogio and of *72* after hearing Barona, more often than you would have done if the series had not been read. The strength of the connection *hear Barona → think of 72* has been changed from approximately zero to a substantial amount. How was this particular change brought to pass, and what in general does the repeated action of a connection between a situation and a response do to that connection?

We may best begin by correcting certain ambiguities in our statements. We have used the word *connection* in two different meanings, and one of them is deplorably vague. When we say that the strength of the connection *Barona spoken → think of 72* has been changed from approximately zero to a substantial amount, we are using the word *connection* clearly as a name for the probability of a certain response occurring very soon after a certain situation; for example, of the thought of *72* occurring after the word *Barona* is spoken. But when we say that we shall investigate the changes produced by the repeated operating of one same connection, *operating of a connection* may mean the mere sequence of two things in time, or such a sequence carrying with it a sense that the second thing belongs with the first, or such a sequence plus the sense of relatedness or belonging and plus also an active production of the second element by the person who is subjected to the first element, or other still more complicated events. The operating of a connection, events happening in connection, connecting or associating *thirty-six* with *four times nine* ten times, and other similar locutions common in psychological discussions, refer to various sorts of connecting or putting things together in the mind which result in the forming or strengthening of a connection in the strict sense of a probability that the one will be closely followed by the other.

Let us consider the potency of repeated connecting of each of these various sorts, beginning with connecting in the sense of mere sequence in the same mind.

If a man simply experiences *A* and *B* in succession repeatedly without any sense that *B* after *A* is right and proper, or even that *B* belongs with *A*, and without himself producing *B* when he suffers *A*, the influence upon the man is very, very slight. You practically always raise the body and bend it back after tying your shoes, and so have the sensations of bending the body back as a sequent to those of tying your shoes. You have done this from say 10,000 to 40,000 times (according to your respective ages and predilections about changing your shoes often), but the experience of tying your shoes has probably never called to mind any sensation, image, or idea of the backward body-bend in one person in 1,000. Mere sequence with no fitness or belonging has done little or nothing.

It is hard to determine experimentally just how little it does, since repeated connecting of any sort with very little attention on the part of the person to what is going on also does very little. And mere temporal contiguity without any sense of belonging or acceptance of the sequence as right or proper often implies inattentiveness or a very low degree of attention to the sequence in question. We need to test mere temporal contiguity, with full or at least average attentiveness.

Our little experiment of a few moments ago * represents

---

* The following sentences were read ten times, the audience being asked to listen to them attentively enough so that they could say that they had heard each word.

> Alfred Dukes and his sister worked sadly.
> Edward Davis and his brother argued rarely.
> Francis Bragg and his cousin played hard.
> Barney Croft and his father watched earnestly.
> Lincoln Blake and his uncle listened gladly.
> Jackson Craig and his son struggled often.
> Charlotte Dean and her friend studied easily.
> Mary Borah and her companion complained dully.
> Norman Foster and his mother bought much.
> Alice Hanson and her teacher came yesterday.

At the end of the tenth reading they were asked to write the answers to these eight questions, being allowed five seconds for each:

1. What word came next after *rarely?*
2. What word came next after *Lincoln?*

an effort in this direction and we may report its results now. By chance alone there should be one in ten correct answers to each question, since the general conditions of the experiment informed you all clearly that the correct answer to the first question was one of the first names beginning the ten sentences and that these were Alfred, Edward, Francis, Barney, Lincoln, Jackson, Charlotte, Mary, Norman, and Alice; and informed you also that the correct answer to the second question was one of the last names and that these were Duke, Davis, Bragg, Croft, Blake, Craig, Dean, Borah, Foster, and Hanson. The number of repetitions of one of the sequences rarely → Francis, gladly → Jackson, and dully → Norman was just the same as the number of repetitions of Lincoln → Blake or Mary → Borah.

In a similar but more careful experiment with ten repetitions of this series of sentences, the per cent correct for a sequence from the end of one sentence to the beginning of the next was 2.75; for a sequence from first to second word in the same sentence it was 21.5. The per cent correct for the word following *and his son struggled often* was 2; for the word following *Norman Foster and his mother* it was 81.*

The series of sentences shown below under "Belonging A" was read six times to 200 college and university students. They were instructed as follows: "Please listen to what I read just attentively enough so that you can say that you have heard it and understood it." As soon as the sixth reading was completed, the subjects were asked to write answers

3. What word came next after *gladly?*
4. What word came next after *dully?*
5. What word came next after *Mary?*
6. What word came next after *earnestly?*
7. What word came next after *Norman Foster and his mother?*
8. What word came next after *and his son struggled often?*

*The results of the experiment made at the beginning of the lecture paralleled these very closely.

to the questions listed below, which were read at a rate of
one every ten seconds in the order shown here.

Belonging A

Alfred	Duke and Ronald	Barnard	worked	sadly.
Edward	Duke and Ronald	Foster	worked	lightly.
Francis	Duke and Ronald	Hanson	worked	here.
Barney	Duke and Ronald	Curtis	worked	to-day.
Lincoln	Davis and Spencer	Lamson	argued	rarely.
Jackson	Davis and Spencer	Evans	argued	singly.
Charlotte	Davis and Spencer	Landis	argued	yesterday.
Mary	Davis and Spencer	Noble	argued	slowly.
Norman	Bragg and Truman	Astor	played	hard.
Alice	Bragg and Truman	Dennis	played	gently.
Daniel	Bragg and Truman	Mason	played	there.
Janet	Bragg and Truman	Napier	played	apart.
Martha	Croft and Roscoe	Bentley	watched	earnestly.
Norah	Croft and Roscoe	Hunter	watched	brightly.
Andrew	Croft and Roscoe	Podson	watched	much.
Ellen	Croft and Roscoe	Conant	watched	late.
Kenneth	Blake and Thomas	Rollins	listened	gladly.
Orville	Blake and Thomas	Durant	listened	everywhere.
Arthur	Blake and Thomas	Roper	listened	then.
Henry	Blake and Thomas	Nichols	listened	long.
Maxwell	Craig and Richard	Allen	struggled	often.
David	Craig and Richard	Franklin	struggled	up.
Laura	Craig and Richard	Travis	struggled	always.
Patrick	Craig and Richard	Custer	struggled	quickly.
Bertram	Dean and Vincent	Ellis	studied	easily.
Norris	Dean and Vincent	Golden	studied	fiercely.
Horace	Dean and Vincent	Wilder	studied	little.
Lewis	Dean and Vincent	Sackett	studied	easily.
Peter	Borah and Sarah	Alden	complained	dully.
Edgar	Borah and Sarah	Hogan	complained	never.
Rachel	Borah and Sarah	Morris	complained	now.
Randolph	Borah and Sarah	Bishop	complained	together.

1. What word came next after *rarely?*
2. What word came next after *much?*
3. What word came next after *up?*
4. What word came next after *fiercely?*
5. What word came next after *Blake and?*
6. What word came next after *Borah and?*
7. What word came next after *Bragg and?*
8. What word came next after *Craig and?*
9. What word came next after *Alfred?*
10. What word came next after *Bertram?*
11. What word came next after *Kenneth?*
12. What word came next after *Lincoln?*
13. What word came next after *Astor?*
14. What word came next after *Allen?*
15. What word came next after *Alden?*
16. What word came next after *Barnard?*
17. What word or words came after *Richard?*
18. What word or words came after *Ronald?*
19. What word or words came after *Roscoe?*
20. What word or words came after *Sarah?*
21. What word or words came after *argued?*
22. What word or words came after *complained?*
23. What word or words came after *listened?*
24. What word or words came after *played?*

Questions 1 to 4 test the strength of the connections from the end of the one sentence to the beginning of the next. Each of these had a frequency of 6 but with very little belonging—only so much as would be due to the few persons who may have considered the series of sentences as something to be memorized as a total. With a possibility of 800 correct responses there were only five, or 0.6 per cent. This number may be accounted for by mere guessing of any given name remembered as having been heard, or even by mere guessing of any common given name.

Questions 21 to 24 test the strength of the connections from verb to adverb in the same sentence. Each verb was followed six times by each of four adverbs. The two terms belonged together closely. With a possibility of 3,200 correct responses (if each subject had written four for each question) there were 265 or 8.3 per cent. Guessing from adverbs remembered would give only eighty, plus or minus a small chance variation, even if each subject wrote sixteen words. As a matter of fact, few of the subjects wrote more than half that number, so that thirty is a generous allowance.

A less extreme contrast between little and much belonging is given by questions 5 to 8 and questions 9 to 12. In the former there were twenty-four occurrences for each of the four connections, but the degree of belonging was only that due to inclusion of the two names in the same sentence. In the latter there were only six occurrences of each connection, but the belonging was of first and last name of the same person in the same sentence.

The correct responses numbered fifty-five for the former and ninety-four for the latter. With only a fourth as many repetitions the greater belongingness results in much greater strengthening, producing nearly twice as many correct responses. In both of these comparisons, position in the test series favors the connections with less belonging.

The principle of belonging is of great importance. It has been neglected by students of learning, perhaps because we have taken it for granted.

A more conclusive experiment may be arranged as follows: Let a long series of pairs of words followed by numbers, like that described earlier, be arranged in which also certain of the numbers are always followed by certain of the words. We announced to the subjects, "I shall read you a long list of pairs of words and numbers like bread 29, wall 16, Texas 78. You will listen as I read them. Pay about as close attention as you would in an average class. Be sure that you hear each pair as I read it." The series of 1,304 pairs contained, among other pairs, four pairs (dregs 91, charade **17,** swing 62, and antelope 35) each occurring twenty-four times, and so placed that

> dregs always came just after 42,
> charade always came just after 86,
> swing always came just after 94, and
> antelope always came just after 97.

After the series had been read, the subjects were asked to write which numbers came just after certain words and also which words came just after certain numbers, namely, 42, 86, 94, 97.

The average percentage of correct response for the numbers following words in pairs occurring eighteen or twenty-one times each scattered throughout the series was 37.5 (median 38). The average percentage of correct responses for the words following the numbers twenty-four times each was 0.5 per cent, which is no more than mere chance guessing would give.

The nature of the instructions, the way in which the pairs were read, and the habits of life in general, led the subjects to consider each word as belonging to the number that followed it, and each number as belonging to the word that preceded it. In this experiment, the temporal contiguity of a number with the word following it, the mere sequence without belonging, does nothing to the connection.

It may be objected that the attentiveness to the *word* → *number* connections inhibits or counteracts a real tendency of the connections from a number to a sequent word to be strengthened by sheer temporal contiguity. But this does not seem to be true. At least, any such tendency is very slight. For if we reduce this alleged inhibition by reducing the attentiveness to that series, we have the same result as before. If, instead of encouraging an attentive and studious attitude to such a series, we instruct subjects, "Do not give any closer attention than is required for you to keep awake and hear the words and numbers," the percentages correct in a second 100 subjects for the *number → word following* pairs are still only what would be attained by chance.

There is one curious and important possible exception to the general evidence that mere sequence in the mind, in and of itself, is very weak and perhaps totally impotent. This possible exception is the so-called conditioning of reflexes, reported first by Pavlov and elaborately studied by his pupils and others, where the act of secreting by the salivary gland of a dog forms a strong connection with the ringing of a bell or the rotating of a disc or the appearance of a black square which repeatedly precedes and overlaps the act of secreting, though presumably the dog feels no fitness or belonging of that act with that situation, and does not produce or control the act, or pay attention to it, or even, perhaps, know that the secreting is taking place.

The work of Pavlov, Beritoff, Krasnogorski, Anrep, and their followers will demand special attention later. Its learning seems to be unlike other learning in several ways. For the present we may leave it as an apparent contradiction to the general evidence that mere temporal contiguity of two events in the mind has little power, perhaps no power, to form a connection between them.

When a psychologist speaks of associating or connecting two things, he ordinarily assumes the feature of belonging. In even so arbitrary a task as learning pairs of names and numbers like *Barona → 72,* Barona and 72 are taken by the learner as belonging together, and indeed as forming a "right" or acceptable sequence, for the experiment at least.

The next feature of importance is the presence of a reaction by the person as the second member of the pair to be connected. It is generally believed by psychologists that if

A and *B* are two words heard in sequence by us, whereas A_1 and B_1 are two words both heard, of which the second is also written by us in sequence, the latter is more efficacious. A situation and an active response to it is something different from two events which we passively experience. In practical pedagogy this distinction is surely of great importance, for it leads to repetitions accompanied by the sense of belongingness, by interest and attention, by locating and curing errors and weak spots, and by reduction of wasteful overlearning. In the fundamental psychology or physiology of learning, it is of less importance, and needs to be expressed in more exact terms. Such words as *active* and *passive* are of little service, and the useful fundamental contrast is not between experiencing and responding. We respond in both cases. In the so-called passive experiencing, what really happens is that the situations are external events, and our responses are the perceptions aroused thereby. The sequence of hearing two words consists of two situation-response pairs, *sound waves → hearing of word A, second set of sound waves → hearing word B.*

In the so-called active responding by hearing two words and ourselves writing the second word, what happens is as before, plus a third situation-response pair, namely, *hearing of word A_1 → writing word B_1.* If the contrast is between hearing *A* and *B* and hearing *A* and recalling *B* from memory, the two events are really as follows: The first comprises two situation-response pairs as before (*sound waves → hearing of A, second set of sound waves → hearing of B*). The second event replaces the second of the pairs by *hearing A → evoking B from memory.* Learning by passive experiencing means in such a case connecting two words by reason of the temporal contiguity of two perceptual responses.

Just what intrinsic advantage the temporal contiguity of

a response to its situation has over an equal temporal contiguity of two neighboring responses, if belongingness and acceptability and attentiveness are present and equal, we need not now inquire. These are the two sorts of connecting one or the other of which is commonly meant when we speak of learning by *frequency* or *exercise* or the *repetition of a connection.*

Repeated connecting of either sort produces learning, though somewhat slowly. I prepared last year a series of about 4,000 pairs like bread 27, door 16, advance 98, in which certain pairs occurred forty-eight times, others twenty-four times, and so on. I selected the pairs; I then wrote out the entire series pair by pair; a week or so later I read three fourths of the entire series to a group in an experiment. I then tested myself with the three pairs which occurred forty-eight times and the ten which had occurred twenty-four times in the series. I had considered the former attentively at least eighty-five times each, and the latter at least forty-three times each. I got one of the three right and three of the ten. Approximately ten minutes after a stenographer had copied the entire list, I asked her to write any numbers that had followed certain of the words, these words being given to her on a sheet. She had none right of the three occurring forty-eight times and only three right of the ten occurring twenty-four times. In my own case, the record was improperly high because in reading the series I sometimes guessed what the number would be as soon as I saw the word and before I saw its number. When I guessed right, the satisfaction of doing so may have strengthened the connection. I also occasionally repeated a pair in inner speech after reading it aloud. On the other hand, the eighty-five or forty-eight or twenty-four repetitions in this experiment are probably weakened by interference from the intervening pairs. Learning would probably be more rapid if the intervals were filled with rest or with less interfering activities. Even so, it would be very slow.

Another individual, an able graduate student and a rapid learner in general, typed a series of 1,208 pairs containing some that occurred from three to twenty-one times each. She did this in the ordinary course of her duties, with no expectation of being tested in any way. Her percentage correct in a test two hours later was 12.5 for the fifteens, eighteens, and twenty-ones taken together. By chance alone she should have had 1.1 per cent.

We have more or less duplicated these natural experiments by concealing the learning under the guise of experiments on fatigue or on lapses. We have also conducted experiments with emphatic instructions not to think about the pairs. The great volume of results so obtained abundantly demonstrates our statement that repetition of a connection plus belonging causes learning, but that the learning is slow. I will quote just one sample. Fourteen adults each wrote 3,586 five-figure numbers dictated in the form "two eighteen ninety-seven, four thirty-two sixteen" as a fatigue experiment. None of them made any effort to remember any of the numbers. As soon as the entire series had been dictated, the subjects of the experiment were given sheets containing many of the numbers read, minus the last two figures. They were required to add the two figures which they remembered as the completion of the three seen in case they did remember them, and to write any two figures that came to mind in case they did not. For numbers which had occurred thirty, thirty-six, forty-two, or forty-eight times in the series, their completions included 5, 5, 3 and 10 per cent correct, as against 1.24 per cent expected by chance.

Repetition of a connection in the sense of the mere sequence of the two things in time has then very, very little power, perhaps none, as a cause of learning. Belonging is necessary. Even when supplemented by belongingness and acceptability it is weak, and seems to need something more to help it account for learning. What this something more may be is the problem for our next discussion.

Lecture 3

THE INFLUENCE OF THE AFTER-EFFECTS OF
A CONNECTION

WE have seen that the repetition of a sequence whose first and second parts are felt as belonging together strengthens the connection leading from the first to the second, though it does so rather slowly. Much of learning seems to involve something more than the mere repetition of relevant sequences. Obvious cases are those where the response which was repeatedly made to a situation in its early occurrences is yet in the end displaced by a response which was very infrequent at the start.

Consider the following experiment: An individual supplies letters to complete a list of 160 words like those shown below. He is to write one letter for each dot.

bet...	f..e	aw.y	p.nt
b..e	dig....	me..	re..
c..ss	fl..t	m.st	r..d
d..n	ju..	min.s	s̩.op
fa...	h..r	v...	wi.e

He does this daily or oftener until he has written the series from sixteen to twenty-four times including sixteen to twenty-four completions of *b.at*. The records of eight individuals for the first sixteen series are shown in Table 4.

The situation, write a letter to make *b.at* into a word, evoked the response of writing *o* in nine out of the first sixteen occurrences (two for each of eight subjects), but by the last sixteen *o* was the response only two times, whereas *l* was the response nine times. As you have doubtless guessed, the consequences attached to writing *o* and *l* were different. By the rules of this particular learning experiment, no letter save *l* was right as a sequent to *b*. When he had written *l* the subject was rewarded by the announcement "Right" by the experimenter. When he wrote *o* he was "punished" by the announcement "Wrong." This is a sample of the many cases which may be observed in the laboratory or in life where frequency competes against the consequences of the connecting and loses.

TABLE 4

LETTERS WRITTEN IN 16 SUCCESSIVE TRIALS TO COMPLETE *b.at*

Subject			
1	o o o o	o e o o	o o o o	o e e l
2	l e l e	l l l l	l l l l	l l l l
3	r o o o	o o l o	e o e o	o e o e
4	o o n o	o e o o	r r l l	l l l l
5	o o o o	r r o r	o l l r	o o o r
6	o o o o	o o l –	l r – o	l l l l
7	r r e o	r r r r	o r o r	o r r r
8	e r e e	e l l l	l l l l	l l l l

Equally important and demonstrative are cases where, at the first occurrences of a situation, each of say five responses has an equal probability (of approximately one in five or 0.20) of being made, whereas in the end one of them has a probability of zero and one a probability of 1.00, that one being the one whose consequence has been a satisfying "Right" compared with the annoying "Wrong" of the others. Any multiple-choice learning which begins with ignorance will serve. For example, subjects learned more or less of a vocabulary of 200 Spanish words arranged as shown below by choosing a meaning and being told "Right" or "Wrong."

1. *abedul*   ameer....birch....couch....carry
....punch   1
2. *abrasar*   oaf....walk....fill....alienate....
burn   2
3. *aceite*   oil....copper....acerbity....crab
....ferment   3
4. *acometer* calculate....asteroid....escort....
attack....credit   4
5. *adefesio* defenceless....relief....nonsense
....support....obstruct   5
6. *adufe*   execution....burning....speechless
....gold-mine....tambourine 6
7. *adunar*   understand....believe....pray....
assist....unite   7
8. *aguante*   watery....chill....want....firm-
ness....serpent   8
9. *alambre* retort....candle....copper....feld-
spar....verse   9
10. *álamo*   prison....poplar....siege....sheep
....tocsin 10

The records of five of them in response to line 1 appear below. Such cases of great strengthening of one connection compared with others of equal or nearly equal initial strength by reason of the different consequences attached to it and to them can be found by the thousands.

RECORDS OF FIVE SUBJECTS IN TWELVE TRIALS OF LINE 1 OF
C I (ABEDUL, ETC.), MADE AT INTERVALS OF FROM
ONE-HALF HOUR TO TWENTY-FOUR HOURS

	1	*2*	*3*	*4*	*5*	*6*	*7*	*8*	*9*	*10*	*11*	*12*
N	5	3	5	3	5	4	1	2	2	2	2	2
P	3	5	4	4	2	2	2	2	2	2	2	2
Ra	4	2	2	3	2	2	2	2	2	2	2	2
Ro	4	1	1	2	2	2	2	2	2	2	2	2
St	3	3	2	1	5	1	5	2	1	2	3	2

How the after-effect of a connecting strengthens or weakens the corresponding connection may well be a matter for dispute, but that it often does so seems to me as sure as the fact of learning itself.

Yet it has been an unpopular doctrine, and various attempts have been made to get along without it. The most promising of these argued that since the connection which led to the "successful" or "right" consequence ended the series of varied responses to the situation, it must always occur at least once per occurrence of the situation, and so would, in the long run, have frequency in its favor, as compared with any one of the "wrong" connections. This argument was unsound as to the facts, because very often a connection which is initially very strong and occurs often is replaced by one initially weak but having favorable consequences.

Kittens put in a box with bars in the front and one and one-half to two inches apart, the door of which falls open when a loop of wire is pulled, will in the first experience try to squeeze through the opening in the front much more frequently than they will pull at the loop. Yet, at the end of forty or fifty experiences, they will almost always pull at the loop of wire, rarely or never attempting to squeeze through the openings. There are many, many similar cases.

Experiments like the one reported with completing words or selecting the right meaning, where each occurrence of the situation produces only one response, the situation being then rewarded, show the error of the assumption that the right response would be more frequent than any other one response. They can readily be arranged so that some wrong response is at the outset far more frequent. For example, subjects were required to estimate in square inches the areas of seventy-four shapes cut out of paper, with the aid of squares of ten, twenty-five, and fifty square inches always present before them, and with announcement of "Right" and "Wrong" after a shape had been judged and removed

TABLE 5

RECORDS OF THE SUCCESSIVE ESTIMATES OF THE AREAS OF CERTAIN SHAPES

The record gives each estimate as a deviation (in square inches) from the correct area. o is thus a correct response.

Sub-
ject Shape   *Successive Estimates*

M   1   −5 −7 −3 −9 −3 −5 +1 −13 −5 −4 −2 −1 0 0 0 0 0−7 −7 0 0 0 0 0 0 0 0 0 0 0

     3   −8 −4 +2 −4 −4 −8 −4 +1 −6 −6 −4 −4 +2 +6 −4 −3 −4 −4 +2 0 +4 0 0 0 0 0 0

     4   −4 −8 −6 −7 −15 −11 +1 −4 −4 −4 −8 −7 −2 −5 −5 −1 −2 −1 −1 0 0 0 0

     9   −5 −5 −7 −5 −3 −9 −7 −3 −3 −7 +5 −7 −1 −5 −5 −1 +3 −1 0 0

   10   −4 −6 −4 −7 −5 −6 −3 0 −1 0 0 0

Shape 1 thus had four −5's before any o, but o prevailed.
Shape 3 thus had four −4's before any o, but o prevailed.
Shape 4 thus had four −4's before any o, but o prevailed.
Shape 9 thus had five −5's before any o, but o prevailed.
Shape 10 thus had three −6's before any o, but o prevailed.

from sight. Table 5 shows the records in cases where some one wrong response occurred much more often than the right response, yet was eventually displaced by the latter.

In Hamilton's experiment with six rats learning to escape by one out of four alleys, there were, in the first two trials, three rats by whom some wrong alley was chosen two or two and one-half times as often as the right one. Two rats chose two or more wrong alleys each as often as the right. Only one rat chose the right oftener than any one wrong alley. Yet all soon came to choose the right alley invariably. (If we use the first trial alone, three rats chose some one wrong alley two or four times as often as the right, one chose a wrong alley as often as the right, and two chose the right alone.)

Yerkes's monkeys Skirrl and Solke in all the harder problems (2, 3, and 4) of his multiple-choice experiment made some one wrong response much oftener than the right response in the first 10 trials, yet they eventually discarded it entirely. The facts are shown in Table 6.

TABLE 6

FREQUENCIES OF THE RIGHT AND THE MOST FREQUENT
WRONG RESPONSE BY THE MONKEYS SKIRRL AND SOLKE
IN THE FIRST SERIES WITH THE YERKES MULTIPLE
CHOICE APPARATUS

			Settings										
			1	2	3	4	5	6	7	8	9	10	Total
Skirrl,	Problem 2	Right	1	1	1	1	1	1	1	1	1	1	10
		Wrong	3	5	5	4	2	1	0	1	2	2	25
Solke,	Problem 2	Right	1	1	1	1	1	1	1	1	1	1	10
		Wrong	8	4	5	5	1	5	1	1	3	6	39
Solke,	Problem 3	Right	1	1	1	1	1	1	1	1	1	1	10
		Wrong	4	1	4	3	5	0	0	1	3	1	22
Solke,	Problem 4	Right	1	1	*	1	*	*	1	*	*	1	5
		Wrong	2	6	*	6	*	*	2	*	*	5	21

* Mastery of these settings was not attained.

I think the unpopularity of the doctrine has been due partly to a prejudice against thinking of the effect of anything as working back upon that thing to cause changes in it, and partly to a reluctance to believe that the effect of a connection influenced it, so long as the mechanism of the influence was a mystery. Both the prejudice and the reluctance should give way in face of the facts.

We have then to learn what sorts of consequences or after-effects of the action of a connection do strengthen or weaken it, and if we can, how they do so. This second question will not, however, concern us during the present lecture.

A first element in this knowledge, justified by the facts, is that many of the consequences which strengthen connections are in the class of satisfiers, a satisfier being defined as a state of affairs which the individual does nothing to avoid, often doing such things as attain and preserve it. Food when hungry, freedom from restraint, hitting the mark, hearing "Right" rather than "Wrong," or being otherwise approved by others or by oneself—these are samples of satisfiers commonly used to aid learning by animals or men. The consequences which seem to weaken connections or strengthen some different connection are all in the class of annoyers, an annoyer being defined as a state of affairs which the animal avoids or changes. Electric shocks, continued confinement, hunger, hearing "Wrong," being disapproved or scorned, perplexity, failure, and shame are commonly used annoyers.

Various experiments have been made to compare the amount of effect of a certain satisfier with the amount of opposite effect of a certain annoyer.

The most important are those of Warden and Aylesworth ['27]. They arranged an apparatus so that if the animals (white rats, three months old) entered a passageway marked by a bright patch of light (from a seventy-five watt "Mazda" bulb), they received an electric shock from a grid on the floor. If they entered a passageway marked by a much less bright patch (unlighted), they received no shock, and, in the case of "reward" experiments, "a nibble of milk-soaked bread."

There were three series of experiments. In the *Reward Series* (*R*), the right response was rewarded and the wrong response was followed by removal of the rats from the goal box and (presumably) transfer to their regular home cage or some resting place. In the *Punishment Series* (*P*), the right response was followed as the wrong one was in the series *R*, and the wrong response was followed by the electric shock and then by removal from the pen and (presumably) transfer as above. In the *Reward and Punishment Series* (*RP*), the right response was rewarded as above and the wrong response was punished as above.

The ten rats of the *Reward Series* learned very slowly, attaining a status of nine right choices out of ten in an average of 293.5 trials. The ten rats of the *Punishment Series* learned much faster, attaining this status after an average of 56.2 trials. The ten rats of Series *RP* learned still faster, attaining the same status after an average of 32.8 trials. A status of eighteen right choices out of twenty was attained by the *P* rats in 104.4 trials, and by the *RP* rats in 59.7 trials. A status of twenty-seven right choices out of thirty was attained by the *P* rats in 145.9 trials and by the *RP* rats in 67.3 trials.

The rats that were punished by the shock responded often thereafter by entering neither passageway, but staying in the reaction chamber. If one did this for five minutes, his trial was counted a failure, and he was removed as above. If the learning task had been *not* to enter the wrong passageway, the punished rats would have surpassed the fed rats even more. The reward-punishment rats may be said to have been taught by the punishment to avoid the wrong passageway and by the reward to avoid staying for five minutes in the reaction chamber, as well as to go to the right passageway.

In such experiments we should consider not only the reward *per se* and the punishment *per se,* but also the reward of the right response as compared with the after-effect of the wrong response and the punishment of the wrong response as compared with the after-effect of the right response. The differential must be considered.

In all considerations of the effect of rewards we probably need to consider also not only the reward *per se* but also the reward in relation to the "set" or "adjustment" of the animal. For an animal set toward obtaining freedom, freedom may have more potency, and food or praise less potency, than these would have if he were set toward obtaining food or favorable attention. In experiments with rats running mazes the satisfyingness of an unimpeded run may outweigh the satisfyingness of eating at the end of it.

The comparative merit of learning by reward and learning by punishment is a matter of such great practical importance that I shall report briefly the results of a recent series of experiments which we have made at the Institute of Educational Research of Teachers College, Columbia University.

We ask the question, "Other things being equal, does one right response to a certain situation rewarded by the announcement of 'Right' strengthen the connection in question more than one wrong response to the situation punished by the announcement of 'Wrong' weakens that connection?"

In an experiment in learning which one of five meanings to choose for a word by repeated choosings, each followed by the announcement of "Right" or "Wrong," we note all the cases among 200 words studied by nine subjects, where the right one of the five meanings printed after each word was chosen in the second and third trial, but not before. We leave out of account all of the cases where the right mean-

TABLE 7

THE COURSE OF LEARNING IN THE FIRST EIGHTEEN RE-
SPONSES TO TWENTY WORDS RESPONDED TO CORRECTLY
IN TRIALS 2 AND 3 BUT NOT BEFORE

1	2	3	4	5	6	7	8	9	10	11	12	13	14	15	16	17	18
x	c	c	c	c	c	x	c	c	c	c	c	c	c	c	c	c	c
x	c	c	c	c	c	c	c	c	c	c	c	c	c	c	c	c	c
x	c	c	c	c	c	c	c	c	c	c	c	c	c	c	c	c	c
x	c	c	c	c	c	c	c	c	c	c	c	c	c	c	c	c	c
x	c	c	c	x	x	x	x	x	x	c	c	c	c	c	c	c	c
x	c	c	x	x	x	x	x	x	x	c	c	c	c	c	c	c	c
x	c	c	c	x	c	c	ċ	c	c	c	c	c	c	c	c	c	c
x	c	c	c	c	c	c	c	c	c	c	c	c	c	c	c	c	c
x	c	c	c	c	c	c	c	c	c	c	c	c	c	c	c	c	c
x	c	c	c	c	c	c	c	c	c	c	c	c	c	c	c	c	c
x	c	c	x	x	x	x	c	c	c	c	c	c	c	c	c	c	c
x	c	c	c	c	c	c	c	c	c	c	c	c	c	c	c	c	c
x	c	c	c	c	c	c	c	c	c	c	c	c	c	c	c	c	c
x	c	c	c	c	c	c	c	c	c	c	c	c	c	c	c	c	c
x	c	c	c	c	c	c	c	c	c	c	c	c	c	c	c	c	c
x	c	c	c	c	c	c	c	c	c	c	c	c	c	c	c	c	c
x	c	c	c	c	c	c	c	c	c	c	c	c	c	c	c	c	c
x	c	c	c	c	c	c	c	c	c	c	c	c	c	c	c	c	c
x	c	c	c	c	c	c	c	c	c	c	c	c	c	c	c	c	c
x	c	c	c	c	c	c	c	c	c	c	c	c	c	c	c	c	c

ing was chosen in the first trial, because in such the right connection may have had an initial strength derived from experiences prior to the experiment. Twenty cases where the responses were right in trials 2 and 3 but not in trial 1 are shown in Table 7. We note similarly all the cases where, in the second and third trials but not before, the same wrong meaning was chosen. Twenty such are shown in Table 8.

TABLE 8

THE COURSE OF LEARNING IN THE FIRST EIGHTEEN RE-
SPONSES TO TWENTY WORDS RESPONDED TO BY SOME
ONE WRONG RESPONSE IN TRIALS 2 AND 3
BUT NOT BEFORE

(o means other than the particular wrong response)

1	2	3	4	5	6	7	8	9	10	11	12	13	14	15	16	17	18
O	X_1	X_1	O	O	O	O	O	O	O	O	O	O	O	O	O	O	O
O	X_1	X_1	O	O	X_1	O	O	X_1	X_1	O	O	O	O	O	O	O	O
O	X_1	X_1	X_1	O	O	O	O	O	O	O	O	O	O	O	O	O	O
O	X_1	X_1	X_1	O	O	O	O	O	O	O	O	O	O	O	O	O	O
O	X_1	X_1	X_1	X_1	X_1	O	X_1	X_1	X_1	O	X_1	O	O	O	O	O	O
O	X_1	X_1	X_1	O	O	O	O	O	O	O	O	O	O	O	O	O	O
O	X_1	X_1	X_1	O	O	O	X_1	X_1	O	O	O	O	O	O	O	O	O
O	X_1	X_1	X_1	O	O	O	O	O	O	O	O	O	O	O	O	O	O
O	X_1	X_1	X_1	X_1	X_1	X_1	O	O	O	X_1	X_1	X_1	X_1	X_1	O	X_1	X_1
O	X_1	X_1	O	X_1	O	O	O	O	O	O	O	O	O	O	O	O	O
O	X_1	X_1	O	O	O	O	O	O	O	O	O	O	O	O	O	O	O
O	X_1	X_1	O	O	O	O	O	O	O	O	O	O	O	O	O	O	O
O	X_1	X_1	O	X_1	O	X_1	O	X_1	O	O	O	X_1	O	O	O	O	O
O	X_1	X_1	O	O	O	O	O	O	O	O	O	O	O	O	O	O	O
O	X_1	X_1	X_1	X_1	O	O	O	O	O	O	O	O	O	O	O	O	O
O	X_1	X_1	O	O	O	O	O	O	O	O	O	O	O	O	X_1	O	X_1
O	X_1	X_1	X_1	O	X_1	X_1	X_1	X_1	X_1	X_1	X_1	O	O	O	O	O	O
O	X_1	X_1	O	O	O	O	O	O	O	O	O	O	O	O	O	O	O
O	X_1	X_1	X_1	X_1	O	O	O	X_1	O	X_1	O	O	O	O	O	O	O
O	X_1	X_1	O	O	O	O	X_1	O	O	O	O	O	O	O	O	O	O

We then compare the two groups, samples of which are shown in Table 7 and Table 8, measuring the influence of two successive correct choices followed by "Right" upon the prevalence of right responses thereafter, and the influence of two successive choices of the same wrong word followed by "Wrong" upon the prevalence of that particular wrong response thereafter.

For example, in the next response following the two

TABLE 9

THE INFLUENCE OF TWO RIGHT RESPONSES REWARDED BY THE ANNOUNCEMENT OF "RIGHT" COMPARED WITH THAT OF TWO OCCURRENCES OF SOME ONE WRONG RESPONSE, PUNISHED BY THE ANNOUNCEMENT OF "WRONG": EXPERIMENT A IN LEARNING THE MEANINGS OF SPANISH WORDS

Number of cases where a right response in the 2d and 3d or 3d and 4th or 2d and 4th trials, but not before, or intervening, was followed in the next trial:

(a) by a right response	174
(b) by a wrong response	73
Per cent which *a* is of *a + b*	70
Per cent due to chance	20
Strengthening due to two connectings in trials 2 and 3, or 3 and 4, or 2 and 4, followed by "Right"	50

Number of cases where a wrong response in the 2d and 3d or 3d and 4th or 2d and 4th trials, but not before, or intervening, was followed in the next trial:

(c) by any other response than it	373
(d) by the same wrong response	137
Per cent which *c* is of *c + d*	73
Per cent due to chance	80
Weakening due to two connectings in trials 2 and 3, or 3 and 4, or 2 and 4, followed by "Wrong"	−7

rights, there were, in our sample of twenty, eighteen rights and two wrongs. By chance there would have been four rights and sixteen wrongs. In our sample of twenty cases with two successive choices of the same wrong word, there were, in the next response, ten instances where that one response did *not* occur, whereas chance would have given sixteen. For the whole group of nine subjects, the facts for the next response following two successive rights or two successive choices of the same wrong (or two such occurring in trials 2 and 4, but not in 1 or 3) were as shown in Table 9. The influence of the "Right" is much stronger than that of the "Wrong."

TABLE 10

THE INFLUENCE OF ANNOUNCEMENTS OF "RIGHT" AFTER A
RIGHT RESPONSE AND OF "WRONG" AFTER A WRONG
RESPONSE: EXPERIMENT A

Number of cases where a right response in the 2d or
3d or 4th trial, but not before, was followed in the
next trial:

    (a) by a right response 283
    (b) by a wrong response 338
Per cent which a is of $a + b$ 46
Per cent due to chance 20
Strengthening due to one connecting in trial 2 or 3 fol-
lowed by "Right" 26
Number of cases where a Wrong response in the 2d or
3d or 4th trial, but not before, was followed in the
next trial:

    (c) by any other response than it 1,609
    (d) by the same wrong response 488
Per cent which c is of $c + d$ 77
Per cent due to chance 80
Weakening due to one connecting in trial 2 or 3, fol-
lowed by "Wrong" .... —3

Table 10 is a similar table, but for the influence of only one right response followed by the announcement of "Right" and only one wrong response followed by the announcement of "Wrong." The response in each case is that made in the second trial but not in the first, or in the third trial but not in the first or second, or in the fourth, but not in the first or second or third.

TABLE II

THE INFLUENCE OF AN ANNOUNCEMENT OF "RIGHT" AFTER EACH RIGHT RESPONSE AND OF "WRONG" AFTER EACH WRONG RESPONSE (EXPERIMENTS A, B, C, D, E, F)

Experiments in Learning to Choose the Right One of Ten Movements

	A	B	C	D	E	F
Number of cases where a right response in the 1st, 2d, or 3d trial, but not before, was followed in the next trial:						
(a) by a right response	283	307	326	10	15	12
(b) by a wrong response	338	171	218	12	8	5
Per cent which a is of $a+b$	46	64	60	45	65	71
Per cent due to chance	20	20	20	10	10	10
Strengthening due to one connecting in trial 1, 2, or 3 followed by "Right"	26	44	40	35	55	61
Number of cases where a wrong response in the 1st, 2d, or 3d trial, but not before, was followed in the next trial:						
(c) by any other response than it	1,609	866	1,272	123	103	108
(d) by the same wrong response	488	365	372	13	17	16
Per cent which c is of $c+d$	77	70	77	90	86	87
Per cent due to chance	80	80	80	90	90	90
Weakening due to one connecting in trial 2, 3, or 4 followed by "Wrong"	—3	—10	—3	0	—4	—3

TABLE 12

THE INFLUENCE OF TWO ANNOUNCEMENTS OF "RIGHT" COMPARED WITH THE INFLUENCE OF TWO ANNOUNCEMENTS OF "WRONG" (EXPERIMENTS A, B, C, D, E, F)

	A	B	C	D	E	F
Number of cases where a right response in the 2d and 3d, or 3d and 4th, or 2d and 4th trials, but not before or intervening, was followed in the next trial:						
(a) by a right response	174	86	234	6	13	10
(b) by a wrong response	73	22	59	0	0	0
Per cent which a is of $a+b$	70	80	80	100	100	100
Per cent due to chance	20	20	20	10	10	10
Strengthening due to two connectings in trials 2 and 3, or 3 and 4, or 2 and 4, followed by "Right"	50	60	60	90	90	90
Number of cases where a wrong response in the 2d and 3d and 4th, or 2d and 4th trials, but not before or intervening, was followed in the next trial:						
(c) by any other response than it	373	132	270	10	14	10
(d) by the same wrong response	137	71	116	5	3	4
Per cent which c is of $c+d$	73	65	70	67	82	71
Per cent due to chance	80	80	80	90	90	90
Weakening due to two connectings in trials 2 and 3, or 3 and 4, followed by "Wrong"	—7	—15	—10	—23	—8	—19

The influence of one "Right" is naturally less than that of two. As in Table 9, an announcement of "Right" strengthens its corresponding connection much more than an announcement of "Wrong" weakens its connection.

We have similar tables from two other extensive experiments in learning to choose the right one from five meanings, and from two experiments in learning to react to ten markedly different signals by ten such movements as reaching forth the right hand, turning the head, nodding, or opening the mouth wide, and from a variant of these.

The general results appear in Tables 11 and 12, and are decisive. Other things being equal, an announcement of "Right" strengthens the connection which it follows and belongs to much more than the announcement of "Wrong" weakens the one which it follows and belongs to.

Indeed the announcement of "Wrong" in our experiments does not weaken the connection at all, so far as we can see. Rather there is more gain in strength from the occurrence of the response than there is weakening by the attachment of "Wrong" to it. Whereas two occurrences of a right response followed by "Right" strengthen the connection much more than one does, two occurrences of a wrong followed by "Wrong" weaken that connection less than one does.

I have studied in the same way the records of the rats, crows, monkeys, and pigs who learned by reward and punishment in the experiments of Yerkes, Kuo, and others. In the case of Kuo's thirteen rats the learning is largely, and perhaps entirely, explainable by the strengthening of the rewarded responses. In the other experiments the relative influence of the rewards and the punishments is not easily measurable, but the former are apparently more potent. I have also supplemented the experiments reported above by additional ones with other subjects and kinds of learning, and have found them fully corroborated.*

These experiments do not, of course, mean that punishment is always futile. The contrary is demonstrable from general observation and from such experiments with animals as those of Warden and Aylesworth. They need not necessarily predispose us to any change of attitude toward punishment save with such learning and for such learners as I have described. But they probably will do so, and probably they should. Since in these experiments with these subjects, the wrong connections were simply displaced or nullified by the right ones, not intrinsically weakened, we may properly expect that something similar may happen in many sorts of learning, and we may increase our confidence in positive rather than negative learning and teaching.

The results of these experiments also lead to important conclusions about the problem of how satisfiers and annoyers do influence connections. Of these I will mention only one. Annoyers do not act on learning in general by weakening whatever connection they follow. If they do anything to learning they do it indirectly by informing the learner that such and such a response in such and such a situation brings distress, or by making the learner feel fear of a certain object, or by making him jump back from a certain place, or by some other definite and specific change which they produce in him. Satisfiers *seem* to act more directly and generally and uniformly and subtly, but just what they do should be studied with much more care than anybody has yet devoted to it.

* The facts are in general too technical to be reported here. They will be published elsewhere.

Lecture 4

EXPLANATIONS OF THE INFLUENCE OF THE
AFTER-EFFECTS OF A CONNECTION

WE have seen that the after-effects of a connection work back upon it to influence it. Our next problem is to learn what we can about how they do so. Facts are rather scanty, and we shall report them in connection with the theories or hypotheses which have been advanced.

The first of these theories declares that they do so by calling up ideas of themselves or of some equivalents for themselves in the mind. For example, in our experiments in learning to choose the right meaning for a word, the person has these experiences: Seeing word *A*, response 1, hearing "Wrong"; seeing word *A*, response 2, hearing "Wrong"; seeing word *A*, response 3, hearing "Right." When he next sees word *A*, any tendency to make response 1 or response 2 calls to his mind some image or memory or ideational equivalent of "Wrong," whereas any tendency to make response 3 calls to his mind some image or memory or ideational equivalent of "Right." So this theory would state. It would state further that such memories or ideas of wrong associated with a tendency must inhibit the tendency, and that such memories and ideas of right associated with a tendency must encourage it to act, and so preserve and strengthen it.

In the same way this theory, which we may call for convenience the representative or ideational theory, would explain the learning of a cat who came to avoid the exit *S* at which it received a mild shock and to favor the exit *F*

47

which led it to food, by the supposition that the tendency to approach and enter S calls to the cat's mind some image or idea or hallucination of the painful shock, whereas the tendency to approach and enter F calls to its mind some representation of the food, and that these representations respectively check and favor these tendencies.

I find two potent objections to any such representative or ideational theory as a general account of the method by which the after-effects of connections strengthen or weaken them. First, the alleged images or memories or ideas of the consequences do not in fact appear often enough during learning.

Sixteen individuals who learned to select the right meaning of a word from five given meanings were asked these questions at the close of the experiment:

1. In learning the meanings of the Spanish words or the rare English words, when you looked at a line after you had had some training but not enough to be sure of the word in that line, what made you think "the first word is wrong, the second is wrong, the third is right"?
   . . . .

2. Was it because the words *right* and *wrong* came to your mind?
   . . . .

3. After you had come to be sure that a certain word was the right one, what made you know that it was right and that the others were wrong?
   . . . .

4. Did an auditory or visual or motor image of the word *right* come in your mind as you looked at the right word on the line?
   . . . .

5. Did an auditory or visual or motor image of the word *wrong* come in your mind as you looked at the wrong words?
   . . . .

Only one of the answers to the first question mentioned guidance by memories of the experimenter saying "Right" and "Wrong," or images of these words. Even when the question was made in the vaguer form and the affirmative answer was suggested, as in question 2, only four answered "yes." One person said "I don't know"; eleven said "No." Not a single answer to the third question made clear mention of guidance by such memories or images. To questions 4 and 5, twelve answered "No," one "Yes," one "Sometimes," and two "I don't know."

In another experiment a dozen subjects estimated the length of strips of paper to the nearest half-inch or quarter-inch, the consequence of each estimate being an announcement of "Right" or "Wrong" by the experimenter. The subjects improved, the connections leading to the right response to, say, a six and one-half inch strip becoming stronger. These subjects were questioned at the close of the experiment as follows: "In learning to estimate the lengths of the white strips, when you looked at a strip and judged it to be, say, eight inches, did there first come to your mind the words *Eight, right?* The fourteen subjects all said "No."

Eight different subjects who learned to estimate the areas of surfaces and were questioned in a similar way gave no evidence save one "Yes" to the most suggestive form of the question.

In learning many acts of skill like swimming, tennis, dancing, or boxing, there not only do not seem to be any such representations of safe progress or of sinking, of the ball's going into or out of the court, and the like, guiding the selection of responses; there does not seem to be any possibility of such being useful, for there is not time. If you stopped to recall the satisfying thud of your fist on your opponent's nose in some previous case as a guide to your blow, you would rarely hit him. In shooting or playing billiards or typewriting, where there could be time, representations still do not appear in most persons on most occasions.

The only cases where I can find any considerable evidence of the guidance of the selection or avoidance of responses by representing to oneself the satisfying or annoying after-effects of previous responses are cases of rather deliberative behavior as in buying at one rather than another store, reading one rather than another author, eating one rather than another food and the like. We may choose to read a book by *A* rather than one by *B* or to order soup *C* rather than soup *D* because of representations of enjoyments called up by the thought of reading *A's* book or eating soup *C*. Even in such cases the predilection for *A* or *C* is perhaps oftener a direct unmediated strengthening of the connection in question. We perhaps oftener just are predisposed toward choosing *A* or *C* without any interposition of a representation of the consequences of past choices.

The second objection lies in the evidence given in the previous lecture that the announcement of "Right" had in our experiments so much greater power to strengthen than the "Wrong" had to weaken the connections in question.

These experiments should be a favored case for the representational theory, since the consequences in the shape of two simple words are easy to represent and to associate. By the representational theory the wrong words should call up the "Wrong" that followed them as often as the right words called up the "Right" which followed them, except for differences in the amount of attention given in the original experiences; and the "Wrong" when called to mind should say "No" to the tendency to choose that wrong word as clearly as the "Right" said "Yes" to the tendency to choose that right word. The announcements of "Right" may have attracted more attention than the announcements of "Wrong," but this difference would not be enough to account for the very great difference in power shown by Tables 11 and 12. That would require by the representative theory that the images or memories of "Right" came to the mind as a result of two announcements of "Right" sixty or more times per hundred, whereas the images or memories of "Wrong" never did.

The next doctrine or hypothesis to be considered is that when a certain connecting has been followed by a satisfier, the individual concerned repeats the connection or something more or less equivalent to it. For example, if he is learning to choose the right meaning for *calamary* from *brocade, squid, gourd, prison* and *flavoring,* and has responded by underlining *squid* and heard "Right," he says in inner speech, *calamary squid, calamary squid.* If he is learning to choose the right movement from ten for each of ten different figures (those shown in Fig. 1) and has responded to a long diagonal by turning his head to the left and heard "Right," he thinks *Long diagonal line, turn head to left.* So this doctrine would affirm. He thus strengthens the right connections himself by repetition. The wrong connections he may simply dismiss, or he may strengthen their negatives as by saying to himself *Four cross lines, don't turn head to left.*

Such strengthening by repetition does, of course, occur in many acts of learning. Everybody must admit that. The question is whether it is the essential and general method by which satisfiers and annoyers following connections strengthen or weaken them, or only an accessory or occasional procedure.

The best way to find the answer seems to be to see what happens in cases where one cannot carry on any such repetition. In many forms of learning skilled acts one cannot. Such are the learning of tennis during actual play, or typewriting or piano-playing during actual performance. A new situation has to be responded to so that there is no time to repeat the successful response.

In the learning of chickens, rats, cats, dogs, raccoons, and the like, there seems small likelihood of any such inner repetition. A rat in a maze obtains freedom to run by turning to the right instead of the left at a certain point;

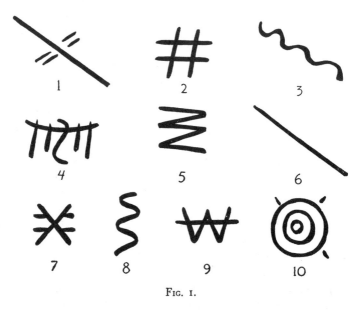

Fig. 1.

and runs on. Does any competent student of rat psychology suppose that it thinks to itself as it runs *At such and such a place, turn right?* A cat in a black box pulls down a loop, and thereby escapes and obtains food. Why should it interrupt its enjoyment of the freedom and food by thinking some equivalent of *Shut up in black box, pull that thingumbob?*

Such considerations as these are perhaps adequate to

negative the repetition of some inner equivalent of the connecting as the cause for its strengthening by a satisfying sequel. But we have tried to make experiments which are crucial for this doctrine and for others as well. The essence of these experiments is to prevent any form of influence by ideas about the connection or by repetition of the connection by having the individuals not know what the connection is. The subject judges which one of four lines is longest. He is instructed as follows: "I shall show you large cards like this. Each has four lines, which we call, beginning at the left, 1, 2, 3, and 4. You will compare the four lines as to length and state the number of the one which you think is the longest. If a line is broken by white strips across it, disregard these and use as its length the distance from one end to the other. The differences in length are very, very small, and consequently your judgments at the beginning may seem to you to be mere guesses." The cards are then displayed; the subject is allowed about five seconds to make his judgment; the experimenter then turns down the card, records the judgment, and announces "Right" or "Wrong."

The series of cards is so constructed that all the differences are utterly indistinguishable, being zero or less than one-half millimeter, but so that in a card which has one line thicker than the others, line 3 is always right. In a card which has one line cut by two white strips, 2 is always right, and similarly for the other sorts of cards used. There is always some feature by connection with which correctness of response can be attained. In a card which has a blot or imperfectly drawn line, line 1 is right, etc., etc. Of all this the subjects know nothing at the start of the experiment, and some of them never learn anything of it. We limit our consideration to them. Of them, some persistently judge by trying to discern some difference in the lengths of the lines after a careful inspection of each of the four.

But this involves a painful eye-strain, and many subjects use the license permitted by the instructions and just give a general look at the card and guess. With the guessing there may be combined various false ideas—that the numbers come in certain sequences, or that the thick line is the longest, or that the line to the right of the line cut by two white strips is the longest, etc., etc. These false ideas do no harm to our experiment.

Whatever the subjects do, so long as they do not learn the right system or any feature of it, the connection between the external situation of a card with one line thicker and the response, "3," will be followed by a "Right," and the connection between that external situation and any other response, of "1," "2," or "4," will be followed by a "Wrong."

But the subjects will not know this and consequently will not repeat to themselves "Card with thick line, 3," after they hear the "Right." If then these subjects learn, that is, improve in their percentage of correct responses, they do so with no aid from inner repetition or rehearsal of the connections which have been followed by satisfiers.

If these subjects do not learn, that will not prove that learning requires repetition. The crucial feature in the external situation may not "belong" sufficiently to the response to be connected with it in the brain. Although the eyes see it, the brain may shunt it off to some limbo for irrelevant elements. But if they do learn, that will prove that learning does not require repetition or rehearsal.

They do learn, and learn more rapidly than subjects who are induced by other means than satisfying consequences to respond correctly to the cards as often as they do.

For example, eight individuals were tested before and after training with announcements of "Right" and "Wrong." Eight others were tested before and after training with no announcement of "Right" or "Wrong," but with the longer line made from one to two and one-half millimeters longer, so that it was judged correctly in a much larger percentage of the trials than in the case of the first eight individuals.

The number of right and wrong responses per person was 590 right and 1,486 wrong for the former or "effect" group, and 618 right and 776 wrong for the latter or "frequency" group. The effect group improved from a total of 362 right to 432 right, or by 19.6 per cent of their early score. The frequency group improved from 371 right to 383 right or by 3.2 per cent of their early score.

Other experiments show smaller differences than this, but the general result of all is in favor of the "effect" groups.

The next hypothesis to be considered is that when a certain connecting has been followed by a satisfier the connection lasts longer than it does when it has been followed by an annoyer. We must distinguish here between two meanings of "the connection lasts longer." It may mean that the situation and response are held together in the mind longer. For example, a person selects squid as the meaning of calamary, keeps *calamary → squid* in mind till he hears "Right" and then continues to keep them in mind, whereas when he selects prison as the meaning of calamary he dismisses or releases *calamary → prison* from his mind as soon as he hears "Wrong." Holding or dismissing thus is comparable to repeating or not repeating; and what has been said about repetition applies. Namely, there is no doubt that such often occurs and facilitates learning, but there is evidence that such holding or dismissing is a common accessory to, rather than a universal and complete cause of, the potency of satisfiers to strengthen the connections which they follow and to which they belong.

That a connection lasts longer may mean that some feature or consequence of the action in the neurones of the brain which is the connection's physiological counterpart lasts longer when it is followed by a satisfier than when it is followed by an annoyer. This might well be true; and could happen in those acts of motor skill, such as actual performance at tennis or typing or playing the violin, where there is no conscious repetition or prolongation of the connection. A beginner at tennis, for example, returns the ball over the net into the court and is satisfied thereby. The game goes on and there is no conscious repetition or prolongation of the situation and response together, but some feature or consequence of the action in the brain which caused the linkage of the latter to the former may conceivably last longer in such a case than in a case where the learner responded to the same situation by popping the ball feebly into the net.

This hypothesis (of prolongation of part of the physiological basis of the connection) has the merit of being simple. Call the physiological counterpart of a connecting C, call the predisposition left by it C_p. Then, other things being equal, if C takes place four times, for .2 second each time, it leaves a greater or stronger C_p. If C takes place for .8 second, it presumably would leave a greater or stronger C_p. Frequency strengthens a connection by adding more C's at intervals. A satisfying sequent strengthens it by adding more C's without a break. The influence of a sequent satisfier is neither more nor less mysterious than that of a repetition. This hypothesis, however, does not easily fit the cases where the satisfiers are delayed for two or three seconds, as, for example, in learning a two-carom or three-carom shot in billiards. This, however, may not be an insuperable difficulty; and all theories have trouble in explaining the influence of long delayed satisfiers.

Another hypothesis for which I myself was responsible fifteen years ago still seems to me to deserve consideration as at least above the level of phantasy.

The hypothesis is, very, very briefly, as follows: The life-processes of a neurone are (1) eating, (2) excreting waste products, (3) growing, (4) being sensitive, conducting and discharging, and (5) movement. The movements or changes of position made by it are restricted to its ends. It may then be, according to its physiological state, more or less ready or unready, disposed or indisposed, to *eat*, to *excrete*, to *grow*, to *play its part in receiving and passing on a stimulus*, and to *move*. Activity in receiving and passing on a stimulus makes it ready to eat. When its life-processes, other than movement, are going on well, it continues whatever movement-activity it is engaged in; when its life-processes, other than movement, are interfered with, it manifests whatever movements such interference evokes until the interference ceases. The movements possible for it are slight extensions or retractions at its ends (including the ends of its collaterals).

The neurone then lives much as would an amœba or paramecium which had been differentiated to make conduction its special trade and which had become fixed immovably save for a few extremities here and there. For the life-processes of eating, excretion, and growth to go on well (or to be interfered with) means much the same in the case of the neurone as in the case of any single-celled animal.

If this hypothesis proved to be correct, the *capacity to learn and remember* could find its physiological basis in the movement-processes of the neurones. A modifiable neurone would, by the hypothesis, maintain that movement-action—and so those spatial relations with other neurones—whereby its life-processes other than movement went on well. Now, for the neurone's life-processes of receiving and transmitting stimuli to go on well in a given state of affairs *is* the physiological fact that we mean when we say that the state of affairs is satisfying to the animal. For this conductive process in the neurones to be interfered with in a given state of affairs is the physiological fact that we mean when we say that the state of affairs is annoying. By the hypothesis, in the latter case the neurones move so as to hold some new spatial relation to neighboring neurones. The neurones are, then, by the hypothesis, widening the gaps in those synapses conduction across which causes discomfort; are trying other spatial relations; and are maintaining those spatial relations—preserving the intimacy of those synapses—conduction across which causes satisfaction.

Each neurone, by so moving as to preserve a healthy condition in its working as a receiving and transmitting organ, would be giving up those synaptic bonds conduction across which produced annoying states of affairs, and maintaining those which produced satisfaction. The law of effect would be a secondary result of the *ordinary avoiding reaction* of unicellular organisms coöperating as elements in the animal's brain. The acquired connections of man's intellect and character would be the result of the unlearned tendencies of his neurones to do nothing different when all was well with them and to perform whatever different acts were in their repertories when their life-processes were disturbed. The learning of an animal would be the product of the unlearned responses of its neurones.

In the above argument I have, chiefly to make a somewhat subtle theory easier to understand, assumed *movement*—spatial change—as a life-process of the neurones. But *any process* whereby the neurone changes the nature of its connections with other neurones will serve all the purposes of the argument. The reader may, for instance, substitute appropriate terms referring to "the greater or less permeability of a membrane" in every case where, in the last two pages, I have used "movement of the end of a neurone." The essence of my account of the physiological mechanism of learning may be stated as follows, independently of any hypothesis about the power of the ends of a neurone to move: The connections formed between situation and response are represented by connections between neurones whereby the disturbance, or neural current, arising in one set of neurones is connected to another set across their synapses. The strength or weakness of a connection means the greater or less likelihood that the same current will be conducted from the former to the latter rather than to some other place. The strength or weakness of the connection is a condition of the synapse. What condition of the synapse it is remains a matter for hypothesis. Close connection might mean protoplasmic union, or proximity of the neurones in space, or a greater permeability of a membrane, or a lowered electrical resistance, or a favorable chemical condition of some other sort. Let us call this undefined condition which parallels the strength of a connection between situation and response the *intimacy* of the synapse. Then the modifiability or connection-changing of a neurone equals its power to alter the intimacy of its synapses.

A neurone modifies the intimacy of its synapses so as to keep intimate those by whose intimacy its other life-processes are favored and to weaken the intimacy of those whereby its other life-processes are hindered. When its feeding, excretory, and conducting processes are going on well, it leaves whatever condition obtains at the synapse, undisturbed. When, on the contrary, feeding, excretion, or conduction is disturbed, it makes whatever changes in its synapses it is capable of. Thus certain synaptic intimacies are strengthened and others weakened, the result being the modifiability of the animal as a whole which we call learning. The simple avoiding reaction of the protozoa, inherited by the neurones of the brain, is the basis of the intelligence of man. The learning of an animal is an instinct of its neurones.

This hypothesis is highly speculative, but it is not mysterious. Such a dynamic of learning could exist and operate, though I can offer no important evidence that it does. It would have the merit of accounting for the influence of repetition of a connection as well as for the influence of having a satisfier as a sequel. I note this fact partly in order to note also that the physiology of the strengthening of connections by repetition is as unknown as the physiology of their strengthening by a satisfier.

There are other physiological theories which perhaps are superior to this one of mine. Like it, they are highly speculative.

Our attempt to find a satisfactory theory of how the consequences of a connection alter it has not been very productive. One reason for this is that we do not know what happens in the neurones when a connection operates and so naturally can only speculate about what happens when it is strengthened or weakened, and can speculate with still less guidance about what happens when it is strengthened or weakened by its after-effects.

One conclusion we may draw with some surety from the evidence which has been brought forward in estimating the various theories. The consequences of a connection seem to act on it directly at the time as well as, or instead of, acting on it indirectly by causing some repetition or rehearsal or reconsideration of it, or by adding some motive or reason for it. Let us examine from this point of view some of the simplest cases of all learning, namely the cases where the same situation persists (or recurs again and again almost immediately after its first appearance). For example, let a young kitten that has never had any experience with fish or meat of any kind be confronted with a row of small flakes of cooked fish identifiable by shape, color, and smell.

It will examine and eat one flake. Another piece is before it, and it repeats the examination (probably abbreviated) and the eating. And so on, so long as it is hungry, with abbreviation of the examination and full retention of the eating. The same kitten confronted in the same way by a row of small friable capsules covered with meat juice but containing weak acid will examine them and may take one into the mouth. It will not repeat the act often, but will soon avoid the capsules. Similarly a dog continues gnawing a bone and discontinues gnawing an object which gives him an electric shock. Similarly we continue to look peacefully at the grass or sky and discontinue looking at a glaring light.

In such learning, one connection is retained, perhaps strengthened, and so acts again and again; the other is soon so weakened that it ceases to act at all for the time being. In either case, the influence of the consequences seems direct. It is fantastic to suppose that the satisfying taste does not in some direct manner validate and confirm the connection which persists or so soon recurs and that the annoying irritation does not directly reject and weaken the connection which is so soon abandoned. Would any students of animal behavior assume that the dog recalled an image of the electric shock and therefore avoided the object? Would any of you testify that you ceased looking at the glaring light because of any image of glare?

Yet, the only difference between the influence of consequences on the connections in such cases and their influence in the stock experiments with animal and human learning is that in the latter the time interval between the successive repetitions of the situation is increased. If the kitten, having been satisfied by taking the first bit of fish, has a stronger tendency to take such a bit of fish a second later (say 20 per cent stronger), the tendency would have been, say, 18 or 19 per cent stronger if the second bit had appeared only after five seconds, and perhaps 15 or 16 per cent stronger if the second bit had appeared only after two minutes. Nothing essentially different should be expected if the interval is two hours. If the strengthening or weakening of the neural bond which is the effective cause of learning occurs in the one case when the satisfier or annoyer occurs, not when we think about it afterward, it must in the latter also. The neurones have no means of telling whether the situation is to persist, or to disappear and recur hours later.

There seems then to be the same sort of direct influence in all cases. In cases where the interval is long, it may be complicated, especially in sophisticated human learning, by various secondary repetitions, judgments, or other forms of inner rehearsal.

So, on the whole, I am compelled to posit a direct influence of the state of affairs which follows a connection and belongs with it upon that connection.

It is high time that I made an apology for the new batch of meanings which have been attached to the word *connection* in these lectures. It has been or will shortly be used to mean at least these eight different things, perhaps more:

1. The probability that a specified situation or first state of affairs in a person will be followed by a specified response or second state of affairs in that person.
2. The occurrence of such a sequence.
3. The occurrence of such a sequence plus the belonging of the response in question with the situation in question.
4. The putting of two things into such a sequence.
5. The putting of two things into such a sequence plus belonging.
6. The condition of the neurones in the brain which corresponds to 1.

7. The action of the neurones in the brain which corresponds to 3.
8. The action of the neurones of the brain which corresponds to 5.

I hope that the context in each case makes what is meant clear enough for the purposes of the argument. We might use *connection* for 1, *sequence* for 2, *sequence plus belonging* for 3, *a connecting in time* for 4, *a connecting in time and process* for 5, *neural bond* for 6, *action of a neural bond* for 7, and *formation of a neural bond* for 8. But these more precise designations for the static and dynamic aspects of connecting and for the events in observed behavior and the physiological bases thereof, would, it seems, do more harm by their uncouthness than good by their freedom from ambiguity. There is after all a real unity in diversity pervading all these uses (or abuses) of the word *connection*. So on the whole we may justify the loose terminology of the past and persist in it. In matters of terminology the most important requirement is that the person conducting the inquiry shall know what he means, so that he will not himself be misled. Whether his meaning in each detail is perfectly clear to those who are trying to learn from him or to refute him is important, but less so. You may rest assured that I shall know what is meant by *connection* in each of the hundreds of times I use the word. If you do not, please complain and order me to specify.

Lecture 5

NEW EXPERIMENTAL DATA ON THE AFTER-
EFFECTS OF A CONNECTION

IN the previous lecture we described an experiment with cards bearing four four-inch lines in which the subjects of the experiment strengthened connections between certain features of the card and tendencies to report the first or second or third or fourth line as longer than the others. This they did without being aware of the connection, and so without any possibility of repeating it to themselves during the learning or calling it to mind as a guide during the test. In such an experiment we have a certain feature of the external situation followed by certain responses each a certain number of times, and with certain specified after-effects controlled by the experimenter, and without interference by inner repetition, rehearsal, or recall by the subject. If we equalize frequency, any balance of strengthening or weakening must be due to the after-effects.

I have tried in the last two years to devise many experiments of this sort, attempting to reduce the danger that some special characteristic of the situation or response would make the experiments unfair tests of the potency of the consequences of a connection to modify it directly.

It is necessary either to have very many subjects with one or two experiments or many experiments each with a moderate number of subjects, because the influence, if there is any, will presumably be very slight, since the connections in question are of a response element with a situation element to which the response does not "belong" at all closely.

A description of some of these experiments and of some of their results will, I hope, give a useful addition to our picture of the dynamics of learning as well as a refutation of the various hypotheses of Hobhouse, Watson, Carr, Woodworth, Tolman, Hollingworth, Peterson, and others which assume that frequency, recency, congruity, facilitation of a consummatory response or of some other form of activity, or the rehearsal or revival in memory of the right response or of its after-effect, is the causal factor.

A subject is trained with vocabulary material of the sort shown below in which he responds by choosing one of the five words and underlining it. As soon as he has done so the experimenter announces "Right" or "Wrong," and the subject proceeds to the next line. The vocabulary material is so arranged that the correct word occurs in positions 1, 2, 3, 4, and 5 counting from the left with relative frequencies of 10, 15, 20, 25, and 30. The training thus connects satisfying after-effects not only with the choices of certain particular words but also with the element of choosing a word toward the right end of the line and the act of underlining at or near the end of a line. Before and after the training the subject was tested with other vocabulary tests than those used in the training.

alguien	somebody...otherwise...goose...shell...blanch
amarillo	crust...hardness...quickly...carbine...yellow
amarrar	love...wed...cover...fasten...injure
amasijo	heap...store...dough...rub...deny
amistad	truce...well being...rain...friendship...loyalty
amolar	teethe...sacrifice...bangle...whisper...sharpen
aquel	par...futile...forgive...that...exact
ara	every...altar...mistake...help...cry
arado	wayside...elm...ditch...plough...emergency
arce	curve...clever...maple...shield...pasture

In some subjects all this happened without any awareness that the right words in the training material were more often in one position than another. In what follows I shall limit the discussion to the records of those subjects.

We can count for each of them the number of times the choice and underlining was of positions 1, 2, 3, 4, and 5 respectively. We can do this either for all responses, or for only those which the individual did not know at the beginning. At the beginning of such learning, the subjects, being entirely at a loss which of the five to choose, more often choose words which come at the beginning of a line. So there may be many trials of the series before the frequency of choice of positions 4 and 5 equals that of positions 1 and 2. We first locate the point of equality in this respect. We then examine the responses to words not yet known at this point, counting how many of them are by underlinings in positions 1, 2, 3, 4, and 5 respectively. We compare these facts with similar ones for the subject's responses at the very beginning of training. Thus subject St at the beginning of training in the case of words of which she was entirely ignorant, underlined positions 1 and 2 in 47 per cent and positions 4 and 5 in 30 per cent of the cases. In trial 16, after training in the course of which the frequency of underlining was nearly the same for 1 and 2 as for 4 and 5 but the frequency of reward much greater for the latter, she underlined positions 1 and 2 in only 23 per cent and positions 4 and 5 in 65 per cent of the cases. Why has she doubled the strength of the tendency to underline 4 and 5 and halved the strength of the tendency to underline 1 and 2?

It cannot be frequency, for she had up to this point underlined 1,209 times in 1 and 2 and only 1,174 in 4 and 5. It might conceivably have been due to a formal system of trying position 1 first, then position 2, and so on until she got

a word right, but an inspection of her records shows that it
was not. She did favor positions 1 and 2, but in no exclusive
or systematic way. The most reasonable explanation is that
she had acquired a tendency, of which she was entirely un-
aware, to choose and underline toward the right end of the
line in positions 4 and 5 because doing so had been rewarded by "right" in 25 per cent and 30 per cent of the
cases compared with 10 per cent and 15 per cent for positions 1 and 2. The sequent "Right" had strengthened not
only the tendencies to underline such and such particular
words, but also the tendency to underline in fourth and fifth
positions.

Before and after the training, the eight subjects were
tested with a similar test-blank containing a hundred different Spanish words. The average number of underlinings in
position 1 falls off from twenty-eight to nineteen; that in
position 5 rises from twelve to twenty-one. The most reasonable explanation of this change is again the strengthening of the tendency to choose and underline certain positions by reason of the satisfying after-effects. It is true that,
by the end of the training, the total frequency of occurrences
of underlinings in positions 4 and 5 had risen above that for
positions 1 and 2. But the following experiment shows that
frequency of choice and underlining without satisfyingness
has little or no power to strengthen connections in such a
case: Eleven individuals were tested in underlining the correct meaning out of five on a line as described above, but
before and after training in which they wrote C after the
correct meaning in each line and underlined whichever word
had a mutilated letter. The correct meanings occurred equally
often in positions 1, 2, 3, 4, and 5 in this experiment, but the
words with mutilated letters occurred 80 times in position 1,
120 times in position 2, 160 times in position 3, 200 times
in position 4, and 240 times in position 5. Since the mutila-

tions were very easily seen, the number of underlinings per position was approximately 80, 120, 160, 200, and 240 per person. There were no announcements of "Right" or "Wrong." The underlinings were no more frequently in positions 4 and 5 after this training than before it.

Other experiments with the influence of satisfyingness upon the position chosen and underlined corroborate these experiments with Spanish words.

Another type of experiment is the following:

The task throughout was to supply one letter for each dot to complete mutilated words like those shown below.

```
ab..
c.ap
d.ve
g..de
gen.s
```

Two hundred and fifty words were used in all. First there was a practice series of 10 words; then there was a test with 40 words; then training with a set of 160 words repeated 14 times or more; then a test with 40 words not used in the initial test or in the training. The two tests of 40 each were selected from 80 by chance to insure substantial equivalence in all essential respects. During the fore-exercise and the initial and final tests, no announcements of "Right" or "Wrong" were made, but during the training there were such announcements. The experimenter followed these directions:

Provide the subject with a pencil. Say, "You will write letters to complete words just as you did before, except that now only certain words will be right. Some letters I shall call wrong even though they make a real word. You will not know at the start on what basis I call certain completions right and certain other completions wrong. And you may never know. You may or may not come to know about it as the experiment progresses. If you get any ideas about it, keep them to yourself. Say nothing to anybody about them. And do not think about these completions at all except when we are experimenting." Then proceed with words 1 to 160 saying "Right" when the right letter is put in place of the first dot and the word is a real word. Say "Wrong" when any other than the right letter is put in place of the first dot. If no completion is made in five seconds, say "Do number ..." (the next in order).

The basis for the announcement of "Right" and "Wrong" during the training was that a dot following an *a* must be filled by a *v*, a dot following a *b* must be filled by an *l*, a dot following a *c* must be filled by an *h*, and so on, with *i* after a *d*, *a* after an *e*, *u* after an *f*, *r* after a *g*, *o* after an *h*, *n* after an *i*, *o* after an *l*, *i* after an *m*, *u* after an *n*, *v* after an *o*, *u* after a *p*, *i* after an *r*, *t* after an *s*, *i* after a *t*, *t* after a *u*, *e* after a *v*, and *r* after a *w*.

Eight subjects were used. Five of them had, by the time of the final test, learned more or less of the basis for the announcement of "Right" and "Wrong." They are not considered in what follows. Three subjects showed by their records in the training and by their negative answers to question 1 and 2, and affirmative answers to question 3 below that they were entirely ignorant of the system.

1. In the learning to complete words by supplying letters, did you come to think that the last letter before the empty space had to be followed by a certain letter? If so, what letter did you think had to come after each of these:

a..	d..	g..	l..	o..	s..	v..
b..	e..	h..	m..	p..	t..	w..
c..	f..	i..	n..	r..	u..	y..

2. In the test at the end did you consciously try to supply right letters; or
3. Did you in the test at the end put in any letters that made a word?

In the test before training, these three subjects had eleven, nine, and eight "right" letters respectively; and in the test after the training, eighteen, nineteen, and ten. Their average gain of 6.3 is about five times its probable error.

An experiment is now being made to discover whether the greater frequency of the right responses during the training had any considerable share in producing this strengthening of the tendencies to think of and write v as a response to a, l as a response to b, h as a response to c, etc. It seems probable that most of the strengthening was due to the satisfying "Right" which followed these connections.

Slips were cut of the same width but of length varying from three to twelve inches by spaces of one-fourth inch. There were two series: a test series in which there were an equal number of strips of each length, and a training series of seventy-three slips in which the "seven" lengths and the "one-fourth" lengths were very frequent.

CONSTITUTION OF THE TRAINING SERIES OF LENGTHS:
NUMBER OF OCCURRENCES OF EACH LENGTH

3	2	5	2	7	4	9	1	11	1
3.25	2	5.25	1	7.25	8	9.25	4	11.25	4
3.5	2	5.5	2	7.5	2	9.5	1	11.5	1
3.75	2	5.75	1	7.75	4	9.75	1	11.75	1
4	2	6	1	8	2	10	2	12	1
4.25	4	6.25	4	8.25	1	10.25	1		
4.5	1	6.5	1	8.5	2	10.5	1		
4.75	1	6.75	1	8.75	1	10.75	1		

The purpose of the experiment was to see whether association would be formed favoring responses beginning with "seven" or ending with "one-fourth," other things being equal. Six subjects were first tested with the test series; they were then trained with the training series in the following manner: A slip was shown; the subject estimated its length to the nearest quarter-inch; the slip was withdrawn from view and the experimenter announced "Right" or "Wrong."

After the experiment was finished the subjects answered the following questions:

1. When you were learning to estimate the lengths of the white strips of paper, did any lengths seem to you to occur especially often?
2. If so, which lengths were they?
3. Did you consciously favor these lengths in the test at the end of the training?

Their answers were:

	q_1	q_2	q_3
M	Yes	6½, 7, 7½	Yes
N	Yes	7¼	Yes
P	Yes	11¼	No
R	No	...	No
Ro	Yes	3	No
Sp	Yes	5 to 8	No

M and N had some awareness of the greater frequency of seven, seven and one fourth, seven and one half, and seven and three fourths. Nobody seemed to be aware of the greater frequency of the "one-fourth" lengths.

We first inquire whether there was an increasing tendency in the *erroneous* judgments in the practice to favor seven, seven and one fourth, seven and one half, and seven and three fourths, and to favor four and one fourth, five and one fourth, six and one fourth, eight and one fourth, nine and one fourth, and ten and one fourth. We compare the first four and second four with the next to last four and last four series, asking how often slips which are really six and one half, six and three fourths, eight, and eight and one

fourth are judged seven, seven and one fourth, seven and
one half, or seven and three fourths.*

We find the following results:

JUDGMENTS OF SIX AND ONE HALF, SIX AND THREE FOURTHS,
EIGHT, AND EIGHT AND ONE FOURTH AS SEVEN, SEVEN
AND ONE FOURTH, SEVEN AND ONE HALF, OR
SEVEN AND THREE FOURTHS

	First	Second	Next to last	Last
M	6	7	10	10
N	4	6	10	12
P	7	6	6	7
R	5	5†	7†	7
Ro	5	7	7	6
Sp	7	8	8	6
Total	34	39	48	48

OTHER ERRONEOUS JUDGMENTS OF SIX AND ONE HALF, SIX
AND THREE FOURTHS, EIGHT, AND EIGHT AND
ONE FOURTH

	First	Second	Next to last	Last
M	14	12	2	4
N	16	11	6	4
P	12	12	10	11
R	13	13†	10†	10
Ro	12	6	5	8
Sp	11	8	7	5
Total	78	62	40	42

† Estimated.

The per cents which the judgments of seven, seven and
one fourth, seven and one half, and seven and three fourths
are of the erroneous judgments of six and one half, six and

* Subject R had only fourteen series, so we use only the first four and
last four in her case.

three fourths, eight, and eight and one fourth thus are for the early series 30 and 39, and for the late series 55 and 53. Without M and N, however, there is much less difference, the per cents being 33, 40, 47, and 43.

We ask also how much oftener in late as compared with early series a slip really four is judged four and one fourth rather than three and three fourths, how much oftener a slip really four and one half is judged four and one fourth rather than four and three fourths, and similarly for the neighbors of five and one fourth, six and one fourth, seven and one fourth, nine and one fourth, and ten and one fourth. We find these results for the first four series, second four, next to last four and last four.

ERRORS OF ¼" "TOWARD" THE "ONE FOURTH" LENGTHS.

	First	Second	Next to last	Last
M	1	10	22	19
N	5	11	14	24
P	5	18	15	7
R	3	3*	10*	10
Ro	1	6	28	15
Sp	1	3	2	2
Total	16	51	91	77

ERRORS OF ¼" "AWAY FROM" THE "ONE FOURTH" LENGTHS.

	First	Second	Next to last	Last
M	1	4	0	0
N	4	17	13	12
P	3	16	9	6
R	10	10*	16*	16
Ro	3	9	4	6
Sp	4	4	0	4
Total	25	60	42	44

* Estimated.

The percentages of errors toward the 'one fourth' lengths are thus 39 and 46 in the early series, and 68 and 64 in the late. Without N, the corresponding per cents are 41, 48, 73, and 62.

There is thus evidence that the subjects acquired tendencies to favor the one fourth judgments toward the end of the practice, though they were not aware of such.

Another set of experiments is illustrated by the following:

The subject was trained to estimate the number of square inches in each of seventy-four pieces of cardboard of varied shapes, and ten, eleven, twelve, thirteen, fourteen, etc., square inches in size. He had before him three squares (of ten, twenty-five, and fifty square inches). The experimenter would show one of the seventy-four; the subject would state his estimate; the experimenter would withdraw the cardboard piece, record the estimate, and announce "Right" or "Wrong." This was continued until the entire series (in a random order) had been displayed and judged. From ten to twenty trials with the series, each time in a new random order, were made.

The series had many of certain sizes and few of others. For example, the sizes from twenty-six on had frequencies as shown below:

26 occurred 1 time			33 occurred 1 time	
27 occurred 1 time			34 occurred 1 time	
28 occurred 6 times			35 occurred 9 times	
29 occurred 1 time			36 occurred 1 time	
30 occurred 2 times			37 occurred 1 time	
31 occurred 7 times			38 occurred 1 time	
32 occurred 1 time			39 occurred 1 time	

TABLE 13

RECORD OF SUBJECT L IN JUDGING AREAS

Response	Occurrences in first two rounds	Occurrences in last two rounds *	All occurrences in intervening rounds	Number of times right in intervening rounds
28	3	5	12	4
31	1	1	8	5
35	5	3	49	42
27	3	1	12	4
29	0	1	9	1
30	12	10	57	6
32	7	6	41	5
34	2	0	5	1
36	3	0	17	3
Total for the three favored	9	9	69	51
Total for the six neighboring not favored	27	18	141	20

* Excluding occurrences as correct responses, since such might be due to special connections with particular shapes.

In what follows we shall consider only the responses to this fraction of the total series.

We compare the subject's wrong responses in the beginning (first two rounds) with his wrong responses in the last two rounds (or rounds 19 and 20, in case the subject had more than twenty rounds of training). We also record the frequency of occurrence of each response (right or wrong) in the intervening rounds.

We have then facts like those shown in Table 13 for each subject, to tell us which tendencies grew stronger from the training, and whether they were the ones with most frequency, or with the most satisfying after-effects. Table 13 shows that sixty-nine occurrences with fifty-one rewardings had more influence than 141 occurrences with twenty rewardings in strengthening (here preventing from weakening) the tendencies to respond by certain sizes, the change being from nine out of thirty-six or 25 per cent to nine out of twenty-seven or 33 per cent in the former and from 75 per cent to 67 per cent in the latter.

For five subjects none of whom reported any awareness that twenty-eight or thirty-one or thirty-five was more frequent in the series than any other size, the totals show a strengthening of twenty-eight, thirty-one, and thirty-five from 20 to 39 per cent by 539 occurrences including 246 rights and a weakening of twenty-seven, twenty-nine, thirty, thirty-two, thirty-four and thirty-six from 80 to 61 per cent by 708 occurrences including sixty-nine rights.

This sort of experiment can be made still more conclusive by using a series like this:

20 occurring 1 time	31 occurring 6 times
23 occurring 6 times	32 occurring 1 time
25 occurring 1 time	34 occurring 6 times
27 occurring 6 times	35 occurring 1 time
30 occurring 1 time	

The subject will pile up frequencies for twenty, twenty-five, thirty, and thirty-five because of the habit of using such round numbers when in doubt, but the satisfying rights will occur much oftener with responses of twenty-three, twenty-seven, thirty-one, and thirty-four. The contrast will then be sharper than in the experiment which I have reported.

In each of these experiments, there is, in addition to the connections which the subject tries to make and knows that he is making, a second connection or set of connections which the subject does not try to make, since in fact he does not know what they are or even, in most cases, that there are any such.

Along with learning to choose the right meaning is this

hidden learning to choose the right-hand end of the line. Along with learning to complete words quickly by supplying omitted letters the subject learns unconsciously to favor *v* after *a, l* after *b, h* after *c,* and so on. Along with learning the areas of certain particular cardboard shapes, he learns to favor certain sizes in general, without knowing that he does so.

The experiments are somewhat delicate to devise and operate, because if the second sort of learning is not well hidden, the subjects will become aware of it. Also if it is carried on to a point where these connections acquire much strength, they may thereby force awareness of themselves. What begins as a direct unconscious strengthening of a connection by its satisfying after-effects may grow into a habit that attracts the subject's attention and then blossoms into a rule of action supported by a judgment.

When this latter happens, the experiment as a whole is spoiled so far as concerns its value as a crucial test of the direct potency of the after-effects of a connection. But it may become a valuable experiment to show that insights not only produce and guide habits but also are produced by them.

I shall use the rest of this lecture in describing one such experiment. A series of 100 pieces of paper was constructed as follows:

> Fifteen pieces of various shapes, but all long and narrow; five of them were nineteen square inches; five were twenty-nine square inches; five were thirty-nine square inches.
>
> Fifteen pieces of various shapes, but all rectangles; five of these were twenty-one square inches; five were thirty-one square inches; five were forty-one square inches.
>
> Fifteen pieces of various shapes, but all rectangles with one corner cut off. Five were twenty-four square inches; five were thirty-four square inches; five were forty-four square inches.

Fifteen pieces of various shapes, but all rectangles plus a triangular addition on top. There were five each of twenty-two, thirty-two, and forty-two square inches.

Fifteen pieces of various shapes, but all rectangles minus a triangular piece cut out from one side. There were five each of sixteen, twenty-six, and thirty-six square inches.

Fifteen pieces of various shapes, but all triangles. There were five each of eighteen, twenty-eight, and thirty-eight square inches.

Ten pieces of very irregular shapes, sizes seventeen, twenty, twenty-three, twenty-five, twenty-seven, thirty, thirty-three, thirty-five, thirty-seven, and forty square inches.

These were displayed one at a time by the experimenter; the subject made his estimate of the number of square inches; the piece of paper was withdrawn by the experimenter and "Right" or "Wrong" was announced by him.

We shall trace the history of Br, a gifted college senior, who in the course of fourteen rounds gained complete understanding that a long narrow strip was always nineteen, twenty-nine, or thirty-nine, and so on for the rest of the system. In the first round she had correct responses as follows:

one 21

one 34 and one 44

two 22's and two 42's

one 18 and one 38

one 26

Long   one 19 and one 29

In her second round she did not get any of these same shapes right except the notched one (twenty-six) and the larger triangle (thirty-eight). She had others right instead, in particular a middle-sized triangle and three more large triangles, making four right out of the five large triangles.

This probably did not happen as a chance series of successes in the general process of estimating. Nor was it the result of a well-defined idea that all big triangles might be thirty-eight and a try-out of this idea. For in the next three rounds the fifth large triangle was judged forty, thirty-seven, and forty-one respectively in spite of the five, nine, and thirteen successes with thirty-eight. Only after successes to the number of seventeen, including sixteen out of the last twenty big triangles judged, did she use thirty-eight uniformly for all. The four successes out of five for the large triangles in the second round were probably due to an imperfect learning by trial and success of the connection, *large triangle* → *thirty-eight*.

In the fifth round, after the seventeen successes with thirty-eight for big triangles, a middle-sized triangle was judged thirty-eight. In the sixth round another middle-sized triangle was judged thirty-eight and in the seventh round after twenty-two successes with thirty-eight for large triangles, every middle-sized triangle except the last one in the series was judged thirty-eight. This perverse response which used thirty-eight repeatedly for a piece of paper obviously very much smaller than the sizes for which thirty-eight had been rewarded as correct, just because consciously or unconsciously thirty-eight had been profitably connected with a triangular shape, is a beautiful illustration of the mixture of habit, reasoning, and prejudice in the thinking of even superior minds.

In the next round (the eighth) Br atoned for this by calling every small triangle eighteen, and every middle-sized triangle twenty-eight. She had previously so called only one out of thirty-five. The hypothesis that triangles were eights was conceived, tried boldly and consistently, and adopted. Thereafter no triangle was ever missed. Perhaps learning painfully by four errors that middle-sized triangles were not thirty-eight may have suggested that they were twenty-eight.

While this was going on in the responses to triangles, Br was also making progress toward the insight that all long, narrow shapes were nineteen, twenty-nine, or thirty-nine. But the process in this case was different. In the first four rounds there was nothing more than the general estimating by size producing four right out of sixty judgments, no piece being judged correctly twice. In the fifth round there was a jump to five right out of fifteen, three of the five being nineteens, i.e., small shapes. In the sixth round the same three nineteens were again judged correctly and three more twenty-nines. In the seventh round these same seven were again judged correctly and also two thirty-nines. Two of the large long, narrow shapes were judged twenty-nine. In the eighth round all the small ones were judged nineteen, all the middle-sized ones twenty-nine, two of the large ones thirty-nine, and the other three twenty-nine. The experience with the triangles had not prevented a repetition of the same neglect of size. The two successes by using thirty-nine and failures by using twenty-nine in the same round sufficed, however, and beginning with the ninth round all long, narrow shapes were correctly judged as nineteen, twenty-nine, or thirty-nine according to their size. Four full rounds including sixty responses were required to develop and establish the insight from its first beginning in the fifth round.

The process in the case of notched rectangles is also instructive. The learning was gradual. The number correct out of fifteen in successive trials was one, one, three, three, one, four, seven, nine, ten, fifteen, fifteen, thirteen, fifteen, and fifteen. In trial seven, although by then the large triangles had been identified as all thirty-eights, and although there had been ten successes with twenty-six for a middle-sized notched rectangle in the first six rounds, and although the first three in the seventh round were safely judged twenty-six, the last two were not. In the eighth trial the twenty-sixes were mastered, but the extension of the principle to the small and large notched rectangles was not fully made until round 10, two rounds after all triangles were mastered and one round after all long, narrow shapes were mastered.

Rectangles with a corner off and plain rectangles were learned in the tenth and eleventh round by a trial and speedy verification of hopeful hypotheses.

Rectangles with a triangle added to one side were barely learned in trial 14. This lateness was due to the fact that Br began to use sixes often for both rectangles with a notch and rectangles with a triangle added to one side in trial 7, and continued to do so until trial 12, although all the successes were with the notched shapes. She did not realize this fact until she had succeeded twenty-six times by using sixes for the notched shapes and failed forty-five times by using them for the added-on shapes. She behaved in this instance like the business man who will not see a gross defect in his business procedure because he is making a good profit. She was gaining in successes with both shapes (from six to seven to nine to ten to fifteen successes), and so "let well enough alone."

The growth of ideas or hypotheses out of mere connections, their verification by success in use and prophecy, their extension by analogies good and bad, the retention of inadequate customs or prejudices in the face of the facts when needed experimentation is neglected, all operating in a mixture of habit and insight—all these appear in this simple experiment.

Lecture 6

IDENTIFIABILITY, AVAILABILITY, TRIAL, AND SYSTEM

I ASK your attention in this lecture to three sets of facts about learning which are important, but which can be treated briefly in description, evidence, and theory. The first set of facts concerns the qualities in a situation which make it easy to connect something with it, and the qualities in a response which make it easy to connect it with something.

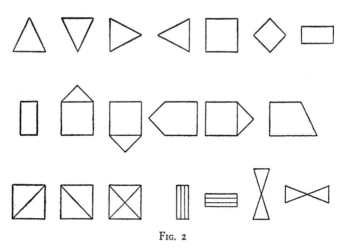

Fig. 2

Consider these two acts of learning, first to connect each of the twenty shapes shown in Fig. 2 with a number from one to twenty, and, second, to connect each of the twenty

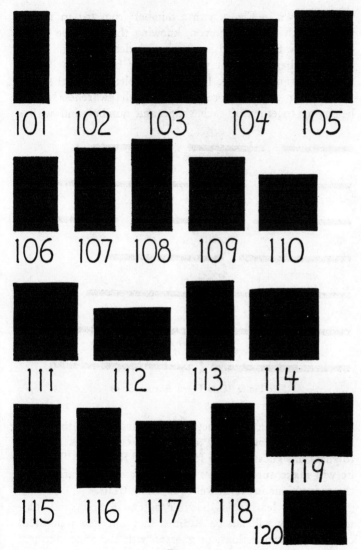

Fig. 3

shapes shown in Fig. 3 with a number from 101 to 120, so that in each case the person, knowing that a shape is one of the given twenty and is to be responded to by one of the given numbers, can tell which number belongs to it. The former learning is easy. If a person is led to say the right number for each a score of times with awareness of the belonging together of each shape and number and with a

Fig. 4 (One Fifth Actual Size)

moderate amount of acceptability attached to the question, he will know many, perhaps all. Or if he is required to guess, his guesses being followed by "Right" or "Wrong," he will make sure progress and master all or nearly all of the connections in from twenty to thirty trials.

The latter learning is hard. Progress is slow, and mastery probably will not be attained in a hundred repetitions of the right connections, or guesses with the announcement of "Right" or "Wrong."

Six educated adults were trained with a series of strips such as are shown in Fig. 4, plus others, the entire series containing strips of three and one half, three and three fourths, four, four and one fourth, and so on to eleven, eleven and one fourth, eleven and one half, eleven and three fourths, and twelve inches. Each subject responded not by a number from 1 to 20, but by saying,

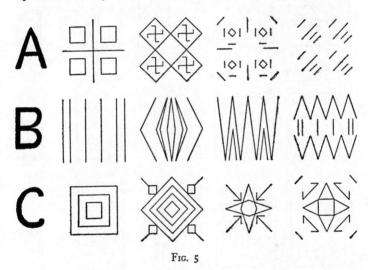

Fig. 5

"Three and one fourth," "Three and one half," "Three and three fourths," "Four," "Four and one fourth," "Four and one half," "Four and three fourths," etc., which presumably made the learning somewhat easier. A strip was laid before him on a 18" × 24" green blotter; he gave his response; the strip was removed; the experimenter announced "Right" or "Wrong." The results for lengths of five, five and one fourth, five and one half, and five and three fourths were as follows for the first fifteen trials: Number correct (out of twenty-four) in successive trials, one, one, six, one, two, four, two, three, seven, four, six, two, three, seven, five. In groups of three we have eight, seven, twelve, twelve, and fifteen right out of seventy-six.

Consider also the learning first to connect each of the twelve shapes shown in Fig. 5 with *A, B,* or *C,* and second

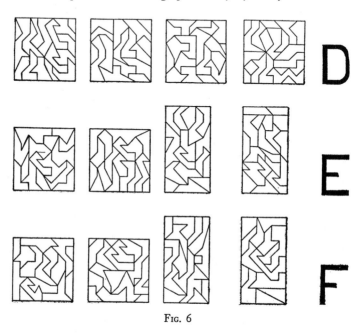

Fig. 6

to connect each of the twelve shapes shown in Fig. 6 with *D, E,* or *F.*

The former is easy. You all have learned it already probably and can give the correct letters for the series in changed order shown in Fig. 7. The latter is hard. If you will repeat the correct connections as shown in Fig. 6 ten times, and then test yourselves with Fig. 8, which gives the shapes in a changed order, few of you will have all twelve correct. (The correct responses are $F, E, F, E, D, D, F, D, E, D, E, F$.)

The greater difficulty of the second task over the first, and of the fourth over the third, illustrates the principle which I have called the identifiability of the situation, that, other things being equal, connections are easy to form in propor-

FIG. 7

tion as the situation is identifiable, distinguishable from others, such that the neurones in your brain can grasp and hold and do something with or to it.

The identifiability of a situation varies according to the brain in question. The shapes of Fig. 2, which are easily identifiable by us, might be elusive to dogs, who in turn may be able to grasp and deal with smells which are elusive to us. To the neurones of trained musicians, chords and timbres may be as identifiable as words are to the rest of us.

Learning as a whole includes changes in the identifiability of situations as well as changes in the connections leading

from them to responses. There are two notable varieties of such changes. First, situations which are hard to identify because they are varying amounts or degrees of some one quality like length, area, weight, brightness, temperature, health, intelligence, and the like are identified by the aid of measurement with scales, crude or refined. Second, elements of situations which are hard to identify because they are hidden qualities or features are analyzed out into relief, and made identifiable by having attention directed specially to them and by the action of varying concomitants and contrast. The results are of very great importance for learning, especially the learning of man. Times, numbers, lengths, volumes, weights, colors, mass, density, force, heat, light, molecules, atoms, nouns, verbs, and the like have to be made thus identifiable before we can profitably learn facts about them. Failures to learn in the school studies are often due to the failure of the brain to get any proper hold of the situation to which the response is to be attached.

Consider now the principle of availability or get-at-ableness of the response, which is that, other things being equal, connections are easy to form in proportion as the response is available, summonable, such that the person can have it or make it at will. Compare these two cases of learning: first to draw with the eyes closed and with one quick shove of the hand a line five inches long (i.e., between four and three fourths and five and one fourth inches long) in response to the situation, the sound of C, and similarly for three, four, six, and seven inches in response to the sounds of A, B, D, and E; second, to touch your left eye with your right hand in one quick movement in response to the situation, the sound of F, and similarly to touch your nose, right eye, right ear, and upper lip in response to the sounds G, H, I, and J, starting the hand always from your right knee as you sit.

The first is very hard to learn, as you can discover for yourselves by getting some one to test you on a pad scaled in inches and quarter-inches, starting your shove always from its left edge and announcing "Right" or "Wrong" to you after each shove. The second is very easy. In ten or eleven trials of the series, *F, G, H, I, J* in changing orders, you will be perfect or nearly perfect.

The responses of moving the hand from the knee to the right ear, right eye, left eye, nose, or upper lip, though much less simple than the shoves of approximately three, four, five, six, and seven inches, are more *available*. Your brain knows what to do to get your hand to your nose; it can do this for you whenever you say so; you can summon the response and connect it with an identifiable situation. But your brain does not know what to do to get your hand to shove a pencil point approximately five inches. After it has done so and been rewarded by "Right" a score of times, it is still far from secure in the performance. You can learn very quickly to give the order for five inches at the situation *C*, three inches at *A*, four inches at *B*, six inches at *D*, and seven inches at *E*, but giving the orders does not get the movements. The difficulty is not in connecting the responses properly with *A, B, C, D*, and *E*, but in getting them at all so that you can connect them with anything. They are not readily summonable or get-at-able.

The slowness of learning due to the unavailability of the response may be illustrated by the following experiment.

The subject was seated, blindfolded, at a table opposite the experimenter, and in front of a drawing board, along the left-hand edge of which a strip of veneer about two inches wide had been fastened in such a way that a large sheet of cross-section paper (16″ × 21″) could be slipped between it and the board and fastened to the board by means of two or three tacks. The strip of veneer served as a fixed starting edge for all lines. The cross-section paper itself was so ruled, in pencil, as to make it possible for the experimenter to tell readily the length of any line drawn from the strip as a zero point.

The subject was instructed to draw lines of a given length,

starting always from the strip of veneer at the left, and to wait after each line until he heard the score called, before drawing the next line. He was required to draw each line with one continuous quick movement.

The subjects were trained to draw three-inch, four-inch, five-inch, and six-inch lines at a single sitting. The number of successive repetitions of a single length varied between four and eight, and the lengths followed each other in a random order, making a series of 600, including 150 of each length. Twenty-four subjects were tested with this series with no announcement of "Right" or "Wrong." They were then trained with the same series, "Right" being announced as the score when a three-inch line was within one eighth of an inch of the correct length and when a four-inch or five-inch or six-inch line was within one fourth of an inch of the correct length. The training lasted seven working days and included thus 1,050 trials of each length.

The per cent of responses which would have been scored right rose from an average of thirteen to an average of twenty-five as a result of 4,200 trials. Two subjects, who continued the training so as to have 21,000 trials in all, increased their percentages of rights to around 90. If the learning had been to put the hand on the right eye, nose, upper lip, and forehead respectively at the signals "Three," "Four," "Five," and "Six," these same subjects would have increased their percentages correct from 0 to 100 in less than one thousandth of this number of trials.

Unavailable responses may be divided into two classes. The first includes such as cannot be made at all, as in the case of moving the ears for most people, (except for special training). The second includes those which, though we make them often, we cannot make to order, as in the case of sneezing or making an approximately exact four-inch shove. Much of the learning of skilled acts consists in changing those of the first class into available responses by learning to make them and to make them to order. Still more consists in changing these of the second class toward greater availability by getting them associated with cues or signals which are available.

The second set of facts which we are to consider concerns features of connections which relate them to purposive thinking, problem-solving, and the like.

A very common type of connection is one in which the situation produces the response of doing whatever is adequate to attain a certain result. For example, the call to dinner in one's home produces different initial movements according as one is standing or seated and different intermediate responses according to where one is in respect to the dining-room. The connection is not from the dinner call to any or all of these movements, but rather to the response of doing what is suitable to reach a certain place. The connection may in such cases be firmly fixed and still be consistent with a large amount of trial, error, and success. For example, to a man desiring to smoke, the situation *A cigar in my mouth* connects strongly with *Light it,* but this simple connection may involve trial and success in searching for a match, in the selection of movements in lighting it, in the provisional movement toward the end of the cigar, and in the final adjustments to get it just at the proper place. Some of these subsidiary movements may be not at all fixed in the connection.

There is thus a mixture of chains of connections of the reflex type and varied reactions with trial and selection by success in even the routines of life, many of these routine connections being, as stated, from a situation to an order to attain a certain goal, rather than from a situation to one particular movement or idea or series of such.

Moreover, we may well believe that, within the brain, what appears to us as a very fixed connection may involve a similar mixture of multiple reaction and selection. When a man fluently repeats the alphabet A, B, C, D, E, etc., his neurones may at each step try several activities and select therefrom by rejecting some and retaining others by virtue of their consequences. We know that even the most fixed connections, like that leading to the knee-jerk, are somewhat variable. We know also that much more time is required for the passage of the current in a simple association or reaction than would be required for its uninterrupted transmission for the given distance in one neurone. It has been common to suppose that this excess time was used up in making a passage across synapses. But part or all of it might be used up in trying several passages before adopting one.

At the other extreme of this process of mixed connecting and selecting are cases where the connection is between a situation and the attainment of a goal which may require hundreds of subsidiary connective and selective activities, and may not be reached for several minutes. More or less of the original situation then remains as a special part of the set of the mind, in subservience to which both the chains of connections and the interspersed selections from multiple responses act. For example, a boy confronts the situation, *Find the product of 435 and 721*. He responds to it by any one of several elaborate procedures, involving many subsidiary situations and responses. *Find the product of 435 and 721* not only starts him on the first step of writing $\frac{435}{721}$ or $\frac{721}{435}$, but also remains as a pervading element and controlling factor during the remainder of the chain, until some status is attained which announces that the required result is attained and bids him turn his mind to other things.

The third set of facts concerns the tendency to make the connections or links or bonds or associative habits which I have represented as the fundamental dynamic features of mental life subservient to certain logical and conventional systems.

Contrast the records of individual S and individual H in an experiment where each received a printed blank like that shown below and was told to follow its directions.

I. E. R.

Copy Line I three times. Then write it, adding one or two strokes to each of the five things. Do not think about what strokes you are to add, but just continue with any movement that you feel like making in each case.

Write the letters of Line II, adding one letter to each of these letters. Do not think about what letter you will add, but just add any letter that you feel like writing.

Write the words of Columns III and IV, adding one word to each of them. Do not think about what word you are going to add, but just add in each case the first word that comes into your head.

III	IV
afraid	on
bread	result
cold	slow
dear	sour
in	tenth
long	wish
needle	working
no	yours

Record of S

bc fg jk om qr ws

III		IV	
afraid	......(illegible)	on	*out*
bread	*butter*	result	......(illegible)
cold	*warm*	slow	*fast*
dear	*friend*	sour	*acid*
in	*out*	tenth	*twelfth*
long	*short*	wish	*long*
needle	*sewing*	working	*rest*
no	*yes*	yours	*mine*

Record of H

bo fi jo on qu wi

III		IV	
afraid	*of*	on	*time*
bread	*and*	result	*of*
cold	*weather*	slow	*motion*
dear	*friend*	sour	*grapes*
in	*summer*	tenth	*commandment*
long	*letter*	wish	*for*
needle	*point*	working	*here*
no	*use*	yours	*truly*

Although writing *b* has almost never been followed by writing *c*, and writing *q* has almost always been followed by writing *u*, individual S writes *bc* and *qr*, being obviously obsessed, as it were, by the alphabetic system. Although *cold warm, in out, long short, no yes,* and *yours mine* have been very rare as temporal connections in hearing, speech, writing, or elsewhere, whereas *cold as, in the, long ride, no thanks and yours truly* have been very common, individual S writes all of the former and none of the latter.

.S is in this experiment ruled by systems. Individual H on the other hand is ruled in large measure by the simpler habitual links. He writes *bo, fi, jo, on, qu, wi.* He writes *afraid of, bread and, cold weather, dear friend, in summer, long letter, no use,* etc.

We may score a response in columns III and IV from 1 to 5 according as it bears fairly sure evidence of simple direct association (scoring 1 for example for *afraid of, on top, no sir,* or *yours truly*), or seems fairly sure to be so (2), or seems doubtful (3), or is probably the result of the influence of some system (4), or is almost certainly so (5) as in *afraid dark, afraid scared, afraid fear, cold hot, cold ice, yours mine.*

The records in such an experiment with a college group will vary from 16 or pure habit to 76 or nearly pure system. The central tendency will be to have nine or ten of the sixteen responses habitual and seven or six of them systematic.

It should be noted that these two influences need not, and usually do not, appear as disparate in the mind of the person who makes the responses. The same individual within the space of a minute may alternate responses of the purely associative and of the systematic sort two or three times. He shifts easily back and forth from the influence of system in *slow fast* to the influence of simple habit in *yours truly* without any sense of shock or awareness of the changing allegiance.

In most cases the addition of *fast* to *slow* seems to him as natural, and even as habitual, as the addition of *truly* to *yours.* Writing *qr* may seem to him as inevitable as writing *qu* does to the person beside him.

The tendency to depart from the beaten track of simple habit in favor of one or another system is very strong, at least in the behavior of persons who are required to reveal their minds in psychological experiments. For example, a stock experiment is to ask people to say or write the first word that comes to mind when a given word is spoken. By the labors of Kent, Rosanoff, and others, we know the frequency with which certain words occur as responses to *afraid, cold, needle* and others of a standard list of 100 words. Roughly speaking, in such experiments, nobody ever says *of* or *that* for *afraid,* or *as* for *cold,* or *and* for *needle,* or *grapes* for *sour,* or *to* for *wish.*

For example, 109 summer-school students took the test shown on page 94, and a day later the Kent-Rosanoff test (given as a group test with approximately five seconds to write a word for each word heard). Seventy-one per cent of them wrote *hot* after *cold,* and none wrote *as.* If they had not been predisposed somewhat to habitual sequences by the previous day's experiment, they would have shown probably an even higher percentage for *hot. Slow* was followed by *fast* in 77 per cent of their records, and by *as* or *down* in none. *Sour* was followed by *sweet* in 63 per cent of their records, and by *as, milk,* and *grapes* in only 0, 0, and 5 per cent respectively. *Afraid of, wish to, wish that, long as,* and *bread and* appear 0, 0, 1, 0, and 0 times respectively.

We may measure the strength of the tendency by the effect of certain stimuli upon it. Thus we may tempt, as it were, the mind away from systematic associations by giving instructions that *the first two or three* words that come to mind be written. This does not have much effect. In an experiment in which forty persons wrote one word and forty others of approximately the same abilities, interests, and tastes wrote two or more words, the number of responses showing simple associations is not much altered. I quote all the cases which show traces of such sequences for *sweet, whistle, woman, cold, slow, wish, river, white, beautiful,* and *window*.

sweet:	like you, potato, apples, girl graduate, as sugar
whistle	for the dog, like a bird, blows hard
woman:	
cold:	winter day, as hell
slow	as the deuce; down girls; moving car
wish:	for better luck; I were home; you were
river:	ran slowly
white:	as snow
beautiful:	as wifie
window:	

We may make an attraction away from systems of things or qualities toward simple connections of habit by putting a word like *a* or *the* or *in* before the stimulus word or by changing its form so as to set the mind more toward the ordinary connections of words.

In the experiment previously mentioned, forty other persons had as the stimuli *the sweet, loud whistle, a woman, very cold, is slow, his wish, deep river, whiter, how beautiful,* and *our window*. I quote the responses showing traces of the influence of direct association and some other relevant facts.

the sweet:	thing (three occurrences); bye and bye; girl. *Pea* and *potato* rise from three to ten occurrences; *sour* drops from eighteen to four.
loud whistle:	of the train; sounds (three). *Blow* (seven) changed to *blow* (two) and *blows* (five) and *blew*.

a woman:	friend, cried, cries, hater (two), knows, plays, reads, scolds, sings (two), smiles.
very cold:	*day, milk, morning, water, weather, wind,* and *winter* rise from three to nineteen occurrences.
is slow:	as, going, molasses, to, to-day, to move, work. *Fast* decreases from twenty-nine to five occurrences; *car, motion, moving,* and *walking* increase from two to eight.
his wish:	came (four), gets, goes, is, to do, to give, to go, was (three). *Desire* and *want* decrease from fifteen to two occurrences.
deep river:	bed, flows (three), runs.
whiter:	than (seven), than snow (two). *Black* and *blacker* decreased from twenty occurrences to two. *Snow* increased from three to nineteen. It seems likely that what was really in the mind in many of these nineteen cases was *than snow.*
how beautiful:	is (four), it, she (three), she is. *Ugly* decreases from sixteen occurrences to one.
our window:	broke, display, opens, overlooks. *Door* and *glass* decreased from fifteen occurrences to three.

These shifts are evidence that the simple connections exist and act. The persistence of such responses to *whiter* as *black, blacker, cleaner,* and *darker* is evidence that the tendency to respond in accordance with systems of things and qualities is very strong. Some of the apparent influence of such systems in association tests is doubtless due to a desire on the part of the subject to make a good impression on the experimenter and on himself and so to being better satisfied by words which are in some logical relation, or seem otherwise relevant or suitable; but I should not assign very much weight to this. Only very rarely, in my opinion, does the subject deliberately desert simple habit in favor of system. Nor should we think that the sharp separation which we have made between simple association and system for purposes of presentation holds always in reality. On the contrary, the influence of simple association and the influence of systems of all sorts often mingle and coöperate intimately in our thinking. My earlier metaphor of "departing from the beaten track of simple habit in favor of one or another system" was not a very happy one. The tracks along which thought moves have been formed by systems as well as by simple habits. There is very little mere connection entirely devoid of organization. On the other hand, these systems, from the humblest such as the alphabet to the proudest such as a science or a philosophy, are themselves constituted out of connections.

Lecture 7

OTHER FACTS CONCERNING MENTAL CONNECTIONS: CONDITIONED REFLEXES AND LEARNING

WE have seen that certain responses become connected with certain situations because of sequence in time, provided the response is treated by the mind (or brain) as "belonging" to the situation and provided the connection of the two has a certain acceptableness or freedom from disfavor. Mere repetition or frequency, in the sense of mere repeated sequence in time, is very weak. As ordinarily used in psychology, the repetition or frequency or use of a connection means sequence in time *plus* belonging. Other things being equal, such use strengthens connections. The chief other thing is the sequel or after-effect or consequence of the connection. This works back upon the connection, satisfiers strengthening it and annoyers often strengthening some alternative connection, opposite to or inconsistent with it. Other things being equal, connections grow stronger if they issue in satisfying states of affairs. Learning, whether by use or effect, is facilitated by identifiability of the situation and by availability of the response.

Such is a first approximate description of a vast amount of learning, including most of the learning of infants and of the lower animals and most of what we call skill and habit in all animals at all ages. In the present lecture I shall supply certain deficiencies in the description and hope to enrich and refine it somewhat.

Hitherto we have always taken, as illustrations of a situation, some state of affairs outside the brain and its end-organs. This was highly desirable so long as we were arguing about changes in the strength of connections, because it prevented or greatly lessened the chance of misunderstandings. But whatever principles of learning apply to connections leading from an external state of affairs to a response of thought or feeling or action probably apply to connections leading from thoughts or feelings to other thoughts or feelings or acts which follow and belong to the former. A situation may be a state of affairs within the brain, as well as a length to be judged, a box to be opened, or a word to be completed. Such inner situations may occur in long series in which situation A evokes B as its response, whereupon B acts as a situation to evoke C as its response, and C in turn acts as a situation to evoke D as its response.

Hitherto we have usually taken, as illustrations of responses, some overt bodily act which could be recorded and measured without dispute, such as saying a word, writing a letter, or shaking the head. But any second term in any connection which we can think of at all can be thought of as the response to the first term which it follows and "belongs" to. If one idea or image or mood or attitude evokes another, and the connection leading from the first to the second becomes stronger or weaker, it probably does so by virtue of the same principles of use, effect, identifiability, and availability by which we learn to fit the most overt acts to the most external situations. The over-zealous type of behaviorist who allows human nature no responses save the acts of muscles and glands is backing the wrong horse. The many hundreds of millions of associative neurones also behave. They do not merely stand and wait, or humbly catch messages from a sensory neurone and toss them to a motor neurone as quickly as may be to get them on out. They can receive and transmit among themselves, and it seems entirely reasonable to suppose that they do.

Among these inner responses are responses of welcoming and rejecting, of emphasizing and restraining, of differentiating and relating, of directing and coördinating other responses. A connection is no less a connection when the things connected are the subtlest relations known by man and the most elusive intellectual adjustments he can make.

The responses of which a human being is capable are not equally ready to act. Eating, sleeping, and looking at bright-colored moving objects are much readier to act than vomiting, walking in one's sleep, or going off into a lonely corner and turning one's face to the wall. The same response is not equally ready to act at all times and seasons. Hunger increases the readiness of eating; weariness makes one unready to play but ready to sleep; being interrupted or diverted in a course of achievement leaves the interrupted response ready to act. We are in fact likely to carry it on in a dream that night. Reaching a satisfactory consummatory reaction leaves the entire course of action temporarily less ready to act.

Of two or more responses equally closely connected with a situation, that one will be more likely to occur which has the higher degree of readiness at the time. A connection may be enormously strong and yet not act because it is at the time very unready. Thus, if a person is made to say "1296758324" 100 times at a signal, he may refuse to say it the hundred and first time from boredom and disgust. On the other hand a certain response may be so chronically ready to conduct that it is evoked by situations which have only very weak connections with it. So, in an egotistical hypochondriac, any mention of any disease will lead him to think of *his* diseases, any mention of any time of day will lead him to think of symptoms which *he* feels at that time of day, any mention of any achievement will lead him to think that *he* would have achieved great things but for his imagined disease. More normally, in all of us, the currents of thought drain into the channels which interest and preoccupation make ready for them.

The readinesses and unreadinesses of certain responses are more or less signaled by certain wants, cravings, annoying lacks, and the like. Whether or not they are so signaled, they help to determine behavior by acting as parts of internal situations, as features of the mind's sets or adjustments, and as responses or parts of responses. The directions for a task, for example, commonly arouse as a response readiness on the part of certain conduction units to conduct as well as the actual activity of certain other units.

Concerning the nature and action of the connections themselves there are many questions to be asked. The first is the one postponed from our second lecture concerning the contrast between the rather weak influence of the mere repetition of a connection which we found in ordinary learning, and the apparently very strong influence found by Pavlov and others in the case of the conditioned reflex.*

The essential facts, as many or all of you know, are as follows:

Dogs are operated on and the opening of one salivary duct is transplanted from its natural place on the mucous membrane of the mouth to the outside skin so that the secretion from one salivary gland discharges into a tube where the amount and rate of the flow can be measured. These dogs are then accustomed to stand in a harness in a room free

* "Conditional reflex," which is, I understand, the correct translation of Pavlov's *ooslovny*, seems much preferable as a name for the fact in question, but I follow the usage of the majority.

from any sights, sounds, or smells save those which the experimenter provides.

By virtue of an inborn or unconditional or unconditioned reflex or tendency, the dog increases the flow of its saliva when certain substances, such as foods or rejectable objects like acid, find their way into its mouth. Suppose now that a certain situation, say, the sound of an electric buzzer, is presented to the animal and while this sound continues, food is presented, and that this connection is repeated daily or oftener a number of times. Then if the sound of the buzzer is presented alone, there will be an increased flow of the saliva. A few repetitions of the series of events shown in Diagram A has created the possibility of the series in Diagram B.

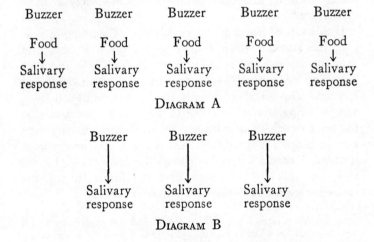

Buzzer	Buzzer	Buzzer	Buzzer	Buzzer
Food	Food	Food	Food	Food
↓	↓	↓	↓	↓
Salivary response	Salivary response	Salivary response	Salivary response	Salivary response

DIAGRAM A

Buzzer	Buzzer	Buzzer
↓	↓	↓
Salivary response	Salivary response	Salivary response

DIAGRAM B

The dog has learned to increase the flow of saliva in response to the sound of the buzzer.

This learning has been hailed by some physiologists and psychologists as a simple, general, fundamental form of modifiability out of which all the complicated forms of animal and human learning are constructed.

The picture which it presents differs from that which we have found in our experiments in several important respects. First, mere sequence and contemporaneity with little or no belonging causes the learning. The food may belong physiologically with the sound, and the increase in the flow of saliva may belong physiologically with the food. But the increase in the flow of saliva can hardly be said to belong with the sound; it simply follows it and goes along with it. Second, there is no demonstrable satisfyingness to the animal as a result of the learning. So far as we can see, he does not profit in any way from secreting more saliva at the sound. Third, a very small number of occurrences usually suffices to bring about the change—sometimes only a single occurrence.*

If this sort of learning is the prototype of learning in general, the account which I have so far given is obviously very incomplete, and it is my duty to show how and why belonging becomes almost a *sine qua non* as it does, and how and why learning becomes so subservient to satisfying and annoying after-effects, and to defend my statement that the mere repetition of a connection strengthens it only very slowly. Indeed, if the conditioned reflex is the prototype of learning, I should not have delayed the description of it till now, but should have put it first and foremost, and described the work of Pavlov and others in detail.

---

* Since this paragraph was written I have had the opportunity to inspect many of Dr. Liddell's unpublished records of behavior in connecting reflex acts to various stimuli and to discuss with Mr. Winsor and Professors Bayne and Kruse the experiments which Mr. Winsor is making on the salivary reflexes in man. It seems probable that I have exaggerated the first and last of the differences. I leave the statement uncorrected, however, because it is such a rapid learning by sheer temporal sequence and contiguity that has been taken to be the prototype of learning.

We should admire the work of these investigators and appreciate its great importance, but we need not be convinced that they are dealing with the fundamentals of all learning. On the contrary, these experiments in which the salivary reflex or some other reflex becomes connected with certain situations seem to me to represent a rather special case. In any case it seems undesirable to discard the reasonable inferences which psychologists have drawn from the behavior and learning of animals and man, and begin all over again, merely because these inferences are not those which have been drawn from the experiments with conditioned reflexes. It seems better to keep both sets of facts and inferences in mind (the *facts* will surely in the end be found to be consistent).

Ignorance of the Russian language and lack of any direct acquaintance with the facts by personal repetition of the classical experiments make me less competent to judge than I would like, and I hope that what I have said and shall say will lead you to study the whole matter and decide for yourselves.

You have on your campus a more competent guide than I in Dr. Liddell, who knows the Russian work intimately and has for several years been conducting important experiments in the formation of connections of this sort in sheep and goats.

Some of the reasons which may justify us in regarding the phenomena of conditioned reflexes as a special case to be put alongside of learning in general, rather than as its fundamental basis and *Anlage,* are stated below. In any case the facts are important.

1. The connections for any given animal usually have one same response or end term, and this is, or becomes in the course of experimentation, very sensitive or excitable. Pavlov writes:

"It was thought at the beginning of our research that it would be sufficient to isolate the experimenter in the research chamber with the dog on its stand, and to refuse admission to anyone else during the course of an experiment. But this precaution was found to be wholly inadequate, since the experimenter, however still he might try to be, was himself a constant source of a large number of stimuli. His slightest movements--blinking of the eyelids or movement of the eyes, posture, respiration and so on—all acted as stimuli which, falling upon the dog, were sufficient to vitiate the experiments by making exact interpretation of the result extremely difficult. In order to exclude this undue influence on the part of the experimenter as far as possible, he had to be stationed outside the room in which the dog was placed, and even this precaution proved unsuccessful in laboratories not specially designed for the study of these particular reflexes. The environment of the animal, even when shut up by itself in a room, is perpetually changing. Footfalls of a passer-by, chance conversations in neighboring rooms, slamming of a door or vibration from a passing van, street-cries, even shadows cast through the windows into the room, any of these casual uncontrolled stimuli falling upon the receptors of the dog set up a disturbance in the cerebral hemispheres and vitiate the experiments. To get over all these disturbing factors a special laboratory was built at the Institute of Experimental Medicine in Petrograd, the funds being provided by a keen and public-spirited Moscow business man. The primary task was the protection of the dogs from uncontrolled extraneous stimuli, and this was effected by surrounding the building with an isolated trench and employing other special structural devices. Inside the building all the research rooms (four to each floor) were isolated from one another by a cross-shaped corridor; the top and ground floors, where these rooms were situated, were separated by an intermediate floor. Each research room was carefully partitioned by the use of sound-proof materials into two compartments—one for the animal, the other for the experimenter." ['27, p. 20 f.]*

Apparently, there develops a pronounced tendency for the reflex to be influenced by any change in the external situa-

* *Conditioned Reflexes* (Oxford University Press).

tion. Learning to salivate at a certain signal may then be more comparable to learning by a little child to do something other than sitting still when a buzzer sounds than to learning to do any particular thing at such a sound.

2. The tendency is extinguished (i.e., vanishes for the time being) very rapidly if it is repeated frequently with short intervals. I quote Pavlov's statement of a typical case:

"In testing the reflex the metronome is sounded for thirty seconds during which the secretion of saliva is measured in drops, and at the same time the interval between the beginning of the stimulus and the beginning of the salivary secretion is recorded. This interval is customarily called the latent period, although, as will be seen later, some other term might more usefully have been employed. Stimulation by the metronome is not followed in this particular experiment by feeding, i.e., contrary to our usual routine the conditioned reflex is not reinforced. The stimulus of the metronome is repeated during periods of thirty seconds at intervals of two minutes. The following results are obtained:

Latent period in seconds	Secretion of saliva in drops during thirty seconds
3	10
7	7
5	8
4	5
5	7
9	4
13	3

. . . "If the experiment had been pushed further, there would have come a stage when the reflex would entirely disappear. This phenomenon of a rapid and more or less smoothly progressive weakening of the reflex to a conditioned stimulus which is repeated a number of times without reinforcement may appropriately be termed *experimental extinction of conditioned reflexes*. Such a term has the advantage that it does not imply any hypothesis as to the exact mechanism by which the phenomenon is brought about." ['27, p. 48 f.]*

Ordinary learned connections do not act in this way. If a child has learned to respond to seven times nine by saying "Sixty-three," and we ask him every two minutes, "How much is seven times nine?" he does not as a rule become more and more halting and inaccurate and, after a dozen repetitions, fail.

3. Such an extinction or temporary weakening and disappearance of the tendency is curable by disuse of the tendency. "Left to themselves, extinguished conditioned reflexes spontaneously recover their full strength after a longer or shorter interval of time" [Pavlov, '27, p. 58].* The contrary occurs with ordinary learned connections, which disuse weakens.

4. The flow of saliva in man is very sensitive, varying readily, as Winsor has shown, in response to chewing, yawning, embarrassment, etc. Yet learning to increase the flow of saliva in response to any originally irrelevant signal is very, very slow in man, so slow that its possibility has even been denied. In ordinary forms of learning man is usually a much more rapid learner than a dog.

5. There are other features of the connection established in a conditioned reflex which do not now seem to have any counterparts in ordinary learning, though more extensive observations and deeper insight may reveal parallelisms.

Thus the temporary extinction of the tendency to respond by saliva flow to the sound of a buzzer by repeating that sound, tends to extinguish also the tendency to respond by saliva flow to any other accustomed signal. This is somewhat as if forgetting that nine times seven is sixty-three made one unable to say that thirty-three plus thirty is sixty-three, or

* *Conditioned Reflexes* (Oxford University Press).

that seventy minus seven is sixty-three. It may even extinguish also the tendency to respond by a defense reaction. This is as if forgetting that nine times seven is sixty-three made one unable to spell *cat,* or to write his own name.

Consider also the following facts: A conditioned reflex $S_1 \rightarrow R$ (R is always the flow of saliva) is firmly established. Then the stimulus is occasionally presented with an addition of S_2, that is, as $S_2 + S_1$. $S_2 + S_1$ is never reinforced by the unconditioned stimulus, food. Then gradually $S_2 + S_1$ evokes R less and less, though S_1 still does so. This occurs only if S_2 and S_1 overlap in time. If S_2 is presented first and removed as soon as S_1 is presented, then S_2 does not so easily weaken the potency of S_1, and the animal is restless. If S_2 is presented and then S_1 after an interval of ten seconds, S_2 causes no weakening of the potency of S_1 and itself acquires a positive potency, evoking R.

Suppose that a delayed conditioned reflex ($S_1 \rightarrow$ specified interval of inactivity followed by R) is established, so that, for example, a touch on the skin is followed in successive half minutes by none, none, two, six, thirteen, and sixteen drops of saliva. If, during the inactive phase of such a delayed conditioned reflex, a stimulus S_2 is added which has never before been connected in any way with the response R, then R appears at once. Two such records from Pavlov are shown below:

Time	Stimulus	Salivary secretion in drops per 30 secs. during the isolated action of the conditioned stimulus
Experiment 1		
9.50 a.m.	Tactile	0, 0, 3, 7, 11, 19
10.03 a.m.	Tactile	0, 0, 0, 5, 11, 13
10.15 a.m.	Tactile + metronome	4, 7, 7, 3, 5, 9
10.30 a.m.	Tactile	0, 0, 0, 3, 12, 14
10.50 a.m.	Tactile	0, 0, 5, 10, 17, 19

Experiment 2

11.46 a.m.	Tactile	3*, 0, 0, 2, 4, 5
12.02 p.m.	Tactile	0, 0, 0, 2, 6, 9
12.17 p.m.	Tactile	0, 0, 0, 2, 7, 9
12.30 p.m.	Rotating object + tactile	6, 4, 6, 3, 7, 15
12.52 p.m.	Tactile	0, 0, 0, 3, 7, 15†

This is as if a dog learned to stand up on his hind legs at approximately sixty or ninety seconds when you said, "Beg in a minute" or, "Beg in a minute and a half," and would do so if nothing else happened, but, if you sneezed or pinched him or did anything else in the meantime, would then promptly stand up on his hind legs. It would be extremely difficult for him to learn the former, and if he did, there is no reason to believe that he would do the latter.

I have hoped for several years to find time and facilities to repeat the classical experiments of the Russian school on primary conditioned reflexes, secondary conditioned reflexes, external inhibition, internal inhibition, conditioned inhibition, delay, etc., paralleling them with connections between similar signals and (instead of the flow of saliva or jerk of the leg) such responses as barking, pawing at a certain object, going to a certain place or pushing down a lever with the nose. If we observe the two sorts of learning side by side, we shall, I think, find that the trial-and-success learning is more important for learning in general than the acquisition of conditioned reflexes. Indeed, I venture, though somewhat timorously, the prophecy that the phenomena of the pure conditioned reflex will teach us more about excitability than about learning.

It is significant that the physiologists and psychologists of the Russian School have used the technique of the conditioned reflex more to explore and explain excitability, inhibi-

___

* "At the 10th second from the beginning of the tactile stimulus the dog moved its leg, striking against a metal basin." [Pavlov, '27, p. 93.]

† *Conditioned Reflexes* (Oxford University Press).

tion, irradiation, induction, and like, than to analyze and prophesy the modifiability of particular tendencies to think, feel, or act in certain ways in certain circumstances.

There is another possibility to be considered. It may be that learning does occur by mere sequence, with or without belonging, very rapidly, if the stream of behavior is narrowed to a single string or series of sequences, and shut off from all the rest of the mind and brain so that there are no competing connections at any point. The conditioned stimulus, 1, the ordinary or unconditioned stimulus, 2, and the response, 3, may by the conditions of the experiment constitute something approximating such a shut-off, insulated system or series so that the brain process of 1 may lead on to that of 3 because that is the only course open to it.

There is some evidence that, in such isolated series, learning is very rapid and forgetting by disuse very slow. A hysterical patient, for example, has an experience which perhaps a year or more later, in a semi-trance state, she relives in its every detail. She does not remember and recall it; she relives it. It is not hooked up with the rest of her mental life. She cannot get any of it at will, but a certain stimulus sets it off and that segment or strand of her life she then and there repeats as before.

I must admit that the reported phenomena of the conditioned reflex are a mystery to me in many respects. Just what their relation to ordinary learning is I do not know, but I am not convinced that they show its fundamental pattern and most general principles.

Our second question concerns the rate of change from 0 strength to 100 per cent strength in the formation of a connection.

Until very recently everybody believed that the change

from approximately o strength of a mental connection to a strength of 100 per cent or stronger * could come gradually, and generally did so come. But recently, partly because of the "all or none" theory of the action of a neurone in conduction, and partly because of the suddenness of the change from no reflex to a clear action of the reflex in the acquisition of a conditioned reflex, it has been suggested that all simple, elementary acts of learning or connection follow the "all or none" law.

The most simple and elementary changes in the connections of the neurones may perhaps act by a leap from o to maximum connectedness. But there seem to be two good reasons for continuing the belief in gradualness for as simple and elementary mental connections as we can observe or conceive. First, any one of them probably involves the simultaneous action of very many neurones. Second, we find gradualness as a fact in the simplest and most elementary connections we can devise.

In our experiments we used striking, very easily identifiable sights, such as those of Fig. 1 (see p. 52), as situations and instinctive or long-familiar acts such as opening the mouth, reaching out the hand, or turning the head to one side, as the responses. There was abundant evidence in the results that such connections were formed gradually. We may be confident that if still simpler and more elementary connections are devised, they will also be formed gradually.**

Acceptability

In an earlier discussion I spoke somewhat vaguely of connections as carrying, or being clothed with, a certain ac-

---

* The reason for the addition of "or stronger" will be found on page 6 f.
** Even in the acquisition of the conditioned reflexes, gradualness may be the rule in the *connection*, the suddenness being due to the response, which does not appear at all until the connection passes a certain minimum strength.

ceptability or disfavor. Some of you may doubt this, or at least object to the imputations of "carrying" and "being clothed with," demanding that they be replaced by "being accompanied by."

I regret that I have no evidence to offer from experiment, but only a few observations. First, a situation with no connection leading to any response save the status of impotence, perplexity, doubt, or despair seems to wear or carry disfavor. Some of you may object that what I really mean is that the impotence, perplexity, etc., wears or carries the disfavor, and that it is a response like any other. That is not what I mean, though it may be what does really happen. What I mean is that the absence of a connection may be an annoying lack as truly as the absence of a certain response or situation. Second, to a mind awake and craving action, the mere process of connecting, regardless of what is connected or produced, seems to carry mild acceptability.

Consider these passages which are the work of a leader in the new art of expression. They are much admired by many, and presumably they were highly acceptable to their author.

"When she was quite a young one she knew she had been in a family and that that family living was one that any one could be one not have been having if they were to be one being one not thinking about being one having been having family living."

And this:

"All there is of more chances is in a book, all there is of any more chances is in a list, all there is of chances is in an address, all there is is what is the best place not to remain sitting, and suggesting that there is no title for relieving rising."

Surely there is nothing desirable in any of the thoughts themselves. The acceptableness which these passages have must reside in the connections, if anywhere!

Third, the acceptability or disfavor which a response incurs often does not attach to the response *per se,* but to it as a resultant or outcome of that situation, that is, to the response plus its connections. For example, suppose you are asked how much nine times fifteen is and reply 145, and hastily correct your response to 135. The disfavor was not incurred by 145, but by 145 as a sequel to "nine times fifteen, how much." This is usually the case in human learning.

Such facts make it unwise to credit the more static features of mental life with a quality of acceptability or disfavor, satisfyingness or annoyingness, but to deny it to the connections between them.

The Attachment of After-Effects to a Connection

How closely must the satisfying or annoying effect of a connection be attached to it by clearness of "belonging" and brevity of time interval, in order that it may have direct influence upon it? No complete or exact answer can be given.* There is reason to believe that the more closely a reward or punishment belongs to the connection, the more influence it has. So, other things being equal, we would expect a dog to learn more quickly to get a bit of meat by pulling a loop if he were rewarded by being allowed to eat the meat, than if he were petted by his master. There is reason to believe that the sooner a reward or punishment comes after the connection acts, the more influence it has. But if nothing intervenes which diverts the influence of the reward from the connection, there probably may be some influence after several seconds. We are much hampered in such inquiries by our ignorance of what connections and belongings are physiologically.

*Dr. Lucien Warner is at present investigating this problem in so far as the time interval is concerned.

Piecemeal Activity and Coöperative Activity

The action of a situation is often differential. That is, some one part or element or feature of it may be prepotent in evoking response. Or, more generally, the parts or elements or features of the same situation may on different occasions have or be given all sorts of different potencies or weights in evoking response. As a result of this piecemeal activity and differential potency, connections are formed not only with gross situations each in its entirety, but also with parts or elements or aspects of situations. A certain part of the total response may be closely bound to one part of the situation and much less closely to other parts. What we call roughly a connection may often really be a bundle of connections. What appears superficially as a connection with a strength of, say, .90 between situation $ABCD$ and response $MNOP$ may in some cases really include also connections such as A to M with a strength of .40, BC to N with a strength of .55, ABD to MNO with a strength of .70, D to $MNOP$ with a strength of .18, AB to $MNOP$ with a strength of .60, A to P with a strength of .05, and many others.

The action of a situation is often coöperative. That is, it produces what result it does by virtue of other situations or elements of situations which have preceded it as well as by its own inherent nature. Its action is, of course, always conditioned by the status or set or adjustment of the mind on which or in which it acts.

As a result of piecemeal activity, differential potency, and determination by both temporary and permanent mental sets, the system of connections in a human mind is complicated almost beyond description. The number of demonstrably different situations which the average person in this room has responded to in the last year is to be reckoned in millions, probably in tens of millions. The system of connections which decided or helped to decide what his responses were is more complicated than all the telephone and telegraph systems in the whole world.

Did these connections decide, or were they only helpers to higher powers—powers of configurations, purposes, insight, analysis, selection, and thought? In the next three lectures, we shall outline the psychology of these so-called higher powers in learning.

Lecture 8

PURPOSIVENESS AND LEARNING: *GESTALT* THEORY AND LEARNING

IT is a general law of mental action that the response to any external situation will depend upon the condition of the person as well as upon the nature of the situation. If the situation is itself an inner one, that is, a part of the person's mind, the response will depend not only on it but also on the rest of him. What a person learns as a consequence of any situation is a consequence of his nature as well.

The condition of the person is conveniently considered as consisting partly of rather permanent and fixed mental sets such as are commonly referred to by the words *instinct, temperament, purpose,* and *ideal,* and partly of more temporary and shifting sets such as are named fatigue, sleepiness, the disposition to add rather than subtract, and the intention to be as unfriendly as is consistent with good manners.

The general fact that the status of the person at the time influences his response is sufficiently obvious, being illustrated by almost every moment of any person's life. More careful and systematic evidence of the choice and direction of connections and the determination of responses by the set or attitude of the person, as influenced by the instructions given him or by the general nature of the task, has been reported by the psychologists who have studied the thought processes.

Equally obvious are the influences of those more permanent attitudes or sets of mind in a person which belong to him as Frenchman or German, Christian or Jew, teacher or physician, father or son, optimist or pessimist, realist or romanticist, extravert or introvert, hard-boiled or sensitive, energetic or inert.

The attitude or set or adjustment of a man is a chief determiner not only of what he thinks and does but also of what he will welcome or reject—of what will satisfy or annoy him. If you are set to speak French, you are discomforted by the thought of an apt English phrase which would have rejoiced you under ordinary conditions. If you are a beginner at golf, you are content with a drive which in later expertness may be intolerable to you.

Every connection is made by a particular person or mind or brain in a particular status. Every after-effect of every connection is an effect upon a particular person or mind or brain in a particular status. Expectations, intentions, purposes, interests, and desires refer to dynamic factors as real as the situation-response connections between hearing *four times five* and thinking *twenty,* or seeing *c a t* and saying "cat."

Some of you have perhaps thought or felt that the view of learning as connecting which I have presented in the previous lectures is too mechanical and fatalistic, leaving no room for the control from within by purposes of the man's own making. Some of my fellow-students of psychology and education certainly think so.

What I have just said concerning the ubiquitous and potent influence of mental sets or dispositions, including the total make-up of the person so far as it may be active in any given case, seems to meet these criticisms.

The influences which coöperate with the situation to determine the response are as complicated, variable, purposive, and spiritual as the learners themselves are. The chief rôle in the drama of learning is not played by the external situations, but by the learner. The reason why I have said much about frequency of connections, satisfyingness of connections, identifiability of situations, availability of responses and the like, and little about the purposes or mental sets or total minds which direct and organize them is not that I belittle the latter. It is rather that the general importance of the latter is obvious, and that the variations of individual idiosyncrasy do not seem specially fruitful for study. So far, then, there should be no quarrel between an honest connectionist or associationist and an honest purposivist. Both equally believe that individual attitudes, adjustments, dispositions, sets, interests, and purposes work with the situations of each moment to determine what connections these shall make.

The quarrel, if any, will be over the connectionist's account of the constitution and development of these attitudes, sets, purposes, or selves.

What is any given set or attitude or disposition of mind made out of? More broadly, what are a person's interests and purposes made out of? Still more broadly, what is his *total mind* or *self* or *entire system of tendencies* that may coöperate with the external situations? The answer which I must in honesty give, though aware of the difficulty which I should have in defending it, is that all these are in the last analysis made out of connections and readinesses, original or acquired, including those multitudinous connections whereby satisfyingness and annoyingness are attached to certain events in the mind.

If I observe any special set or purpose, such as the tendency to divide rather than multiply, or the desire to give opposites rather than meanings, or the lust for fame, or patriotism, or general benevolence, and list what I find in it, the list contains ideas, connections with totals and with elements, readinesses to connect, interests, and the like—all produced by original tendencies or past connectings and rewardings. If I attempt to analyze a man's entire mind, I find connections of varying strength between (a) situations, elements of situations, and compounds of situations and (b) responses, readinesses to respond, facilitations, inhibitions, and directions of responses. If all of these could be completely inventoried, telling what the man would think and do and what would satisfy and annoy him, in every conceivable situation, it seems to me that nothing would be left.

I read the facts which psychologists report about adjustments, configurations, drives, integrations, purposes, tensions, and the like, and all of these facts seem to me to be reducible, so far as concerns their powers to influence the course of thought or feeling or action, to connections and readinesses. Learning is connecting. The mind is man's connection-system. Purposes are as mechanical in their nature and action as anything else is.

I shall not defend this doctrine. It will be more interesting and broadening to use the time at our disposal to present a doctrine which is, or at least is supposed to be, in sharp contrast with the connectionism which these lectures have presented.

Gestalt-Theory and Learning

What I shall say about Gestalt-theory and learning will probably be unsatisfactory to its advocates, partly because of necessary brevity and incompleteness, and partly perhaps because of inability on my part to understand it. I hope at least to be neither unfair nor misleading.

Gestalt-theory is a protest against three extreme forms of psychological atomism, and a constructive doctrine of the organization of mental life. (1) It denies that a state of mind consists simply and solely of a sum or mosaic of elements, an enumeration of which would state all that one needs to know or can know about that state of mind. It declares that the whole mental state is more than an additive combination of these parts, having a pattern or configuration or form not reported by their enumeration, and that the parts when in such a state of mind are not as they would be when out of it, or in some other state of mind, each being modified by the community.

(2) It denies that a given part or element of condition or action in the brain, say, conduction through neurone A and across the synapse to neurone B, will always produce the same result, asserting that this will depend upon what the condition of other neurones is, and upon what other neurones are acting at or near the time and how they are acting. The total result of a complex brain activity is not then predictable by knowledge of what each part of it would produce if active alone. It declares that there are physiological patterns or configurations, having a potency beyond that of the sum of the potencies of their parts. Koffka, for example, writes that "association may be explained in terms of the physical configurations of the nervous system," and that "these configurations . . . will now prove of special value in clarifying the achievements of intelligence." ['25, p. 236.]

(3) It denies that a longitudinal segment of behavior, say, writing *cat* when asked to do so, or putting on one's coat when one feels cold, or reciting the alphabet, or responding to "What is the product of nineteen times seventy-eight?" by the necessary computations, consists simply and solely of certain elements of thought, feeling, and action in a certain sequence. It declares that such a segment or strand or flow of behavior often has, or rather is, also a configuration or pattern, or several such. It is not beads connected by various clasps, but a necklace. It is not a series of tones,

but a melody. It is not men walking in a column, but a procession.

The first of these three pairs of denials and assertions has relevance to the psychology of learning in two ways. First, it emphasizes the general difficulties of any too simple theory of learning by the addition of elements. This will be brought out even better by the third denial and assertion, and will be considered later. Second, it directly exposes the special difficulties of explaining the learned or acquired element in perception by certain exaggerated and perverted forms of the traditional British associationism, according to which, for example, the mind first got yellowness, circularity, solidity, four-inch-diameter-ness, orangy taste, and orangy odor, and then put them together to perceive an orange. This seems as unnecessary and fantastic to an associationist or connectionist of to-day as it does to Wertheimer, Köhler, Koffka, or Ogden.

I have deliberately omitted any discussion of learning to perceive objects and events from this series of lectures in order to save time for matters which seemed to me more important, and I shall consequently say no more about *Gestalt* theories of perception and learning to perceive.

The denial that a given small fraction of status or action in the brain always produces the same result and the assertion that there are physical patterns or configurations in the brain with powers over and above the powers of the conductions and connections and other elementary facts in the neurones which are in the pattern are important. We want a psychology of learning which is in harmony with the facts which are known or are likely to be learned about the action of the neurones. The connectionist frankly admits that his belief in the influences of sequence in time, belongingness, and satisfying consequences in making one state of affairs more likely to evoke another rests not only on observations of behavior, but also on the probability that learning in general is caused by modifiability in the paths which conduction follows in the neurones. He frankly admits that his explanations of abstraction and generalization, though chosen because of observations of behavior, are made more attractive to him because they require from the neurones nothing beyond growth, excitability, conductivity, and modifiability.

I regret that I cannot give evidence for or against the alleged physiological configurations or discuss them usefully. For I cannot imagine at all clearly what they are supposed to be. I cannot tell wherein the configurative brain-process which makes a person find the opposite of a given word differs from that which makes him find the product of two given numbers, except that one is the x which produces the one result and the other is the y which produces the other result. I cannot even tell whether they are composed of conductions in neurones, or of something else, or of conductions plus something else.

The connectionist welcomes the factual criticisms of an over-simplified conduction system made for example by Köhler, and hopes that the study of the organization of thought and conduct by gifted psychologists may lead to advances in knowledge of the organization of brain action. The connectionist, indeed, realizes the difficulties of explaining human nature as a system of connections between neurones perhaps even more clearly and acutely than the Gestaltist does. But on the whole, he finds reason to think that it is being and will be so explained. Stresses and strains, equilibria, and other qualitative features sometimes attributed to the physiological configurations, do not seem hopeful to him. He is also somewhat suspicious of them because for a time they were offered as a substitute for psycho-vitalism. Vitalism in the case of learning (or anything else) is likely in practice to be an abandonment of science, a cowardly retreat to causes whose action is unpredictable and uncontrollable by man. We do not want it or anything like it.

The connectionist welcomes the labors of a Franz or a Lashley which cast doubt on certain theories of the localization of cerebral functions. He is glad to support any competent worker who explores the possibilities of theories of selective resonance or the like as substitutes for the doctrine of spatial proximity of axones to dendrites or of permeable synapses. He will suffer gladly criticism on the factual level. But when he is told by speculative vitalists, "Thus far shall neurone action go and no further; the remainder of learning is due to vital forces, above and beyond any mechanism," he pays no attention. He is too busy, for instance in studying neurology or biophysics.

The third denial and assertion are, of course, the most important for our purpose. The denial that a piece of behavior is fully described by stating what thoughts and feelings and acts are in it and what order they have should encourage or force all students of behavior and of the modifications in it which we ascribe to learning to more careful observations and more thorough analysis. The assertion that the unit of behavior is, often or always, a configuration or pattern subject to the principle of closure, and tending to become as clear and definite as possible, is a challenge to show a better theory of organization within the situation-response sequence.

The denial seems correct and wise. Human behavior is not an undifferentiated series of events. Much of it falls into units longitudinally, each with a beginning and an end. Suppose, for example, that a child is playing with his blocks, that you approach and offer him a bit of cooky, that he reaches for this, grasps it, puts it in his mouth, and continues to play. The fraction of the behavior beginning with his awareness of your offering and ending with his deposit of it in his buccal cavity has a genuine unity. It is a pattern or configuration, if you please, set off against a ground, akin in a real sense to other units in form, though the offerer, the thing offered, the position of the child, the exact nature of the reaching movements, the grasping, and the insertion may not duplicate exactly any previous sequence. If we call the states outside the child from the first instant of his awareness of the offering to the end, the situation, and call what he does from that first instant until he returns to his play again, his response, it is true, as Ogden writes, that "situation and response operate together as one unit, the general pattern of which as it unfolds itself is constantly conditioned by subtle variations both in the situation and in the organic readiness for response." ['26, p. 49]. The behavior sequence *playing with blocks → awareness of mother with cooky* is genuinely different from the sequence just described. It leads on to something new rather than back to the *status quo ante*. It ends in something reasonably called suspense, a problem, or a tension, rather than in something reasonably called a result or a resting phase. It does not so obviously begin and end.

Much of the stream of life is made up of such little unitary dramas as the child's awareness of the person with food and his response thereto, set off, by breaks in belongingness, from the *status quo ante* and the *status quo post* and set up in relief above the minor contemporaneous events. But not, I think, all. There are spells of shorter and less coherent sequences and also very long series of sequences related not as the parts of a configuration to its total, but as incidents in a general plan, or as steps in a useful routine, or even as connections coöperating by little more than addition.

If the units with beginning and end into which the behavior of a man often divides itself are all to be called configurations, that term must be made so elastic as to be well-nigh useless. Consider three of the commonest behaviors of our lives—conversing, driving automobiles, and, more rarely, walking. A friend says, "Whom are you going to vote for on Tuesday?" and you reply, "I think that probably I shall vote for Hoover, but I am not sure." Responding to the sound of *whom* uttered after a pause and with a certain inflection by a sense of impending inquiry *in re* some person is a unit of a sort. Responding to "are you going" by certain ideas and readinesses is a unit of a sort. Responding to "Whom are you going to vote for?" by understanding it is a unit of a different sort, with more finality to its end. Responding to "on Tuesday" by understanding it is a unit of a still different sort, with more finality to its end than the behavior to "Whom" or "are you going," and with much less internal complexity and interdependence of parts than the behavior to "Whom are you going to vote for?" Responding to the entire question by the entire answer is a unit of a still different sort. Responding to the total status up to the moment of saying "probably" by saying it is a unit of a still different sort. Some of these units conform fairly well to the specifications of a *Gestalt* or configuration; some do not, for example, the *understanding "whom"* unit, or the *understanding "on Tuesday"* unit, or the *saying "probably"* unit.

A man is driving his automobile. During much of the time there are no obvious divisions into longitudinal units. He is set or adjusted or disposed toward driving the car, and he maintains certain rather steady responses of posture, grip, and pressure on the gas, varying these slightly so as to maintain the satisfyingness of going at the desired speed on the right side of the road. It seems pedantic to cut up a minute of such driving into a dozen separate units. The state of affairs is rather a smooth flow. It is only when he sees a hill, or tries to pass a car ahead, or slows up for a turn that we have states of affairs usefully thought of as having beginnings and ends.

A man is walking home from work, with his mind set to get home. Some units are obvious, as when, arriving at corner A, he turns to the left, or as when, arriving at a cross street, he stops and looks up and down for traffic. Some are important, though not so obvious, as when the situation-changes of each footfall release the motor action of the next step forward, right and left alternating with probably not one mistake in 10,000. When the effects of the mile of walking produce an increase in fatigue or thirst or a reduction in nervousness, we have a very important situation-response connection which may begin and grow and wane and vanish by infinitesimals.

Turning a corner and seeing whether a street is safe to cross can be treated as configurations, but such situation-response units as ordinary walking displays seem too mechanical and such situation-response units as the reduction of nervousness seem too lacking in form.

In general, few of the units into which behavior may be divided are configurations in the strict sense of things "the unitariness of which defies analysis," which "are transposable like melodies," and which "when they appear or disappear do so altogether." [Ogden, '26, p. 127.] A heard or a seen word calling up its meaning and a person or object calling up its name are two of the commonest units or cases of "belonging" with clear beginning and end, but each of these *is* analyzable and is *not* transposable. It seems therefore extreme to assert as Koffka does that "all learning requires the arousal of configural patterns," or that "repetitions without the achievement of a configuration remain ineffective whenever they are not positively harmful," or that, "In the broadest sense, practice means the formation of a figure rather than the strengthening of bonds of connection." ['25, p. 235.] The configurationist is in a stronger position when he accepts the formation of connections as the explanation of much learning, reserving configuration to be a principle of organization.

Learning the symbols of shorthand, the vocabulary of a foreign language, to smile under this, that, and the other discomfiture, to add more rapidly, to typewrite, to judge lengths or to draw lengths more accurately—these are samples of thousands of sorts of learning where the unity is the simple belonging of situation and response, not an unanalyzable *Gestalt*.

Dynamically, configurations and closure are invoked to do certain things in behavior supposed to be too hard for a certain sort of connection-system, namely, one made up by the mere addition or subtraction of sequences, and perhaps to be too hard for any system of connections. The configurations are supposed to change the man by establishing and perfecting themselves, tending by some inner power to become as good and as sharply defined as possible.

I hope that the sort of connection-system which I have described in these lectures is more acceptable than the kind against which configurationists like Köhler and Koffka and Ogden direct their criticisms—criticisms from which I have profited, and with which I often agree. We have seen that the influence of belonging is as genuine as that of frequency or repetition. We have seen that one very common type of connection is that between a situation and an order to attain a certain result, the subsidiary connections by which that result is attained being left undetermined. We have seen that a process of varied reaction with selection and weighting of tendencies very often is intermingled with the routines of habit. Few or no habits are absolutely "fixed." Even reaching for the spoon that is always at the right of one's plate at breakfast contains a quantum of exploration with guidance by sight or touch or both.

We have seen that even a rather simple segment of behavior may display a subtle, piecemeal activity of situations and an elaborate coöperation of connections.

We have seen that connections are treated differently according to their acceptability and their consequences. Connections which thwart the man's purpose are rejected and replaced by others. Satisfyingness is not a deity invoked occasionally to select a few exciting and crucial connections. It is constantly at work, getting food safely into our mouths, keeping our handwriting up to a certain standard of legibility, and guiding almost every sentence that we speak.

The connectionist theory of life and learning, a summary account of which I have given, is doubtless neither adequate nor accurate. Its explanations of purposive behavior, abstraction, general notions, and reasoning are only a first and provisional attack on these problems. It has many gaps and defects. But I cannot see that such a connection-system requires aid from closure or *Prägnanz*. The facts which they explain seem explainable nearly or quite as well by varied reaction guided by the satisfyingness of the results attained, and this seems far simpler and more in accord with what the neurones are and can do.*

* This lecture was written and delivered before the publication of Köhler's *Gestalt Psychology* ['29]. I have profited from this most recent presentation in many ways, but it seems best to leave the lecture unaltered.

Lecture 9

IDEATIONAL LEARNING

IT has been customary to contrast such learning as is usually found in the acquisition of skills by man or in the majority of acquisitions of any sort by animals below the primates with such learning as is found in the solution of novel intellectual problems by man. The former is called *associative learning* or *learning by trial and error* (*trial and success* is a more fitting name); the latter may be called *learning by ideas*.

In our discussions so far we have not needed to make this contrast. The situation-response formula is adequate to cover learning of any sort, whether it comes with ideas or without, conscious or unconscious, impulsive or deliberate, by natural forces, by *Gestalten,* or even by a miracle; and the facts about belonging, acceptability, repetition of a situation, repetition of a connection, the influence of satisfying and annoying consequences, the identifiability of the situation, and the availability of the response, are presumably as true when ideas are the responses as when anything else is. But the contrast obviously deserves attention, if only because of its importance in the history of psychology.

The contrast as ordinarily used has not depended upon a rigorous definition of ideas, and we may best defer and perhaps altogether avoid such. We all recognize in a vague and general way the difference between a boy learning to swim in the days before swimming teachers or books about swimming, and the same boy learning to solve "If three times a number plus half of the number is twenty-one, what is the number?"

The contrast in the case of animal learning may be illustrated by the earliest account of the trial-and-success learning of kittens and by Köhler's account of how chimpanzees learn to draw food nearer to their cage by using a stick. In 1898 I wrote of the kittens:

"The behavior of all but 11 and 13 was practically the same. When put into the box, the cat would show evident signs of discomfort and of an impulse to escape from confinement. It tries to squeeze through any opening; it claws and bites at the bars or wire; it thrusts its paws out through any opening and claws at everything it reaches; it continues its efforts when it strikes anything loose and shaky; it may claw at things within the box. It does not pay very much attention to the food outside, but seems simply to strive instinctively to escape from confinement. The vigor with which it struggles is extraordinary. For eight or ten minutes it will claw and bite and squeeze incessantly. With 13, an old cat, and 11, an uncommonly sluggish cat, the behavior was different. They did not struggle vigorously or continually. On some occasions they did not even struggle at all. It was therefore necessary to let them out of some box a few times, feeding them each time. After they thus associate climbing out of the box with getting food, they will try to get out whenever put in. They do not, even then, struggle so vigorously or get so excited as the rest. In either case, whether the impulse to struggle be due to an instinctive reaction to confinement or to an association, it is likely to succeed in letting the cat out of the box. The cat that is clawing all over the box in her impulsive struggle will probably claw the string or loop or button so as to open the door. And gradually all the other non-successful impulses will be stamped out and the particular impulse leading to the successful act will be stamped in by the resulting pleasure, until, after many trials the cat will, when put in the box, immediately claw the button or loop in a definite way." ['98, p. 13.]

Köhler writes of the chimpanzees Tschego, Nueva, and Koko as follows:

"She [Tschego] is let out of her sleeping-place into the barred cage in which she spends her waking hours; outside the cage and beyond the reach of her exceptionally long arms, lies the objective; within the cage, somewhat to one side, but near the bars, are several sticks.

"Tschego first tries to reach the fruit with her hand; of course, in vain. She then moves back and lies down; then she makes another attempt, only to give it up again. This goes on for more than half an hour. Finally she lies down for good, and takes no further interest in the objective. The sticks might be non-existent as far as she is concerned, although they can hardly escape her attention as they are in her immediate neighborhood. But now the younger animals, who are disporting themselves outside the stockade, begin to take notice, and approach the objective gradually. Suddenly Tschego leaps to her feet, seizes a stick, and quite adroitly, pulls the bananas till they are within reach. In this manœuvre, she immediately places the stick on the *farther* side of the bananas. She uses first the left arm, then the right, and frequently changes from one to the other. She does not always hold the stick as a human being would, but sometimes clutches it as she does her food, between the third and fourth fingers, while the thumb is pressed against it, from the other side.

"Nueva was tested three days after her arrival (11th March, 1914). She had not yet made the acquaintance of the other animals but remained isolated in a cage. A little stick is introduced into her cage; she scrapes the ground with it, pushes the banana skins together into a heap, and then carelessly drops the stick at a distance of about three-quarters of a metre from the bars. Ten minutes later, fruit is placed outside the cage beyond her reach. She grasps at it, vainly of course, and then begins the characteristic complaint of the chimpanzee: she thrusts both lips—especially the lower—forward, for a couple of inches, gazes imploringly at the observer, utters whimpering sounds,* and

* As is well known the chimpanzee never sheds tears.

finally flings herself onto the ground on her back—a gesture most eloquent of despair, which may be observed on other occasions as well. Thus, between lamentations and entreaties, some time passes, until—about seven minutes after the fruit has been exhibited to her—she suddenly casts a look at the stick, ceases her moaning, seizes the stick, stretches it out of the cage, and succeeds, though somewhat clumsily, in drawing the bananas within arm's length. Moreover, Nueva at once put the end of her stick behind and beyond the objective, holding it in this test, as in later experiments, in her left hand by preference. The test is repeated after an hour's interval; on this second occasion, the animal has recourse to the stick much sooner, and uses it with more skill; and, at a third repetition, the stick is used immediately, as on all subsequent occasions. Nueva's skill in using it was fully developed after very few repetitions.

"On the second day after his arrival (10. 7. 1914), Koko was, as usual, fastened to a tree with a collar and chain. A thin stick was secretly pushed into his reach; he did not notice it at first, then he gnawed at it for a minute. When an hour had elapsed, a banana was laid upon the ground, outside the circle of which his chain formed a radius, and also beyond his reach. After some useless attempts to grasp it with his hand, Koko suddenly seized the stick, which lay about one metre behind him, gazed at his objective, then again let fall the stick. He then made vigorous efforts to grasp the objective with his foot, which could reach farther than his hand, owing to the chain being attached to his neck, and then gave up this method of approach. Then he suddenly took the stick again, and drew the objective towards himself, though very clumsily." ['25, pp. 31-34.]*

Among the criteria of learning by ideas, one of the most satisfactory is the suddenness of the change from total inability to mastery. This change is sometimes represented by a sudden rise in the percentage of successes from what chance would give to approximately 100, and sometimes by a sudden drop in the time required to select the right response to a situation.

* Köhler, *The Mentality of Apes* (Harcourt, Brace and Company).

As samples I quote from my experiments with monkeys reported in 1901.

"The difference between these records and those of the chicks, cats and dogs given on pages 18-26, 33-34 and 37 of the 'Animal Intelligence' is undeniable. Whereas the latter were practically unanimous, save in the cases of the very easiest performances, in showing a process of gradual learning by a gradual elimination of unsuccessful movements, and a gradual reinforcement of the successful one, these are unanimous, save in the very hardest, in showing a process of sudden acquisition by a rapid, often apparently instantaneous, abandonment of the unsuccessful movements and a selection of the appropriate one which rivals in suddenness the selections made by human beings in similar performances. It is natural to infer that the monkeys who suddenly replace a lot of general pulling and clawing by a single definite pull at a hook or bar have an idea of the hook or bar and of the movement they make. The rate of their progress is so different from that of the cats and dogs that we cannot help imagining as the cause of it a totally different mental function, namely, free ideas instead of vague sense impressions and impulses. But our interpretation of these results should not be too hasty. We must first consider several other possible explanations of the rapidity of learning by the monkeys before jumping to the conclusion that the forces which bring about the sudden formation of associations in human beings are present." ['01, p. 15 f.]

"My experiments on discrimination were of the following general type: I got the animal into the habit of reacting to a certain signal (a sound, movement, posture, visual presentation or what not) by some well-defined act. In the cases to be described this act was to come down from his customary positions about the top of the cage, to a place at the bottom. I then would give him a bit of food. When this habit was wholly or partly formed, I would begin to mix with that signal another signal enough like it so that the animal would respond in the same manner. In the cases where I gave this signal I would not feed him. I could then determine whether the animal did discriminate or not, and his progress toward perfect discrimination in case he did. If an animal responds indiscriminately to both signals (that is, does not learn to disregard the 'no food' signal), it is well to test him by using two somewhat similar signals, after one of which you feed at one place and after the other of which you feed him at a different place.

"If the animal profits by his training by acquiring ideas of the two signals and associates with them ideas of 'food' and 'no food,' 'go down' and 'stay still,' and uses these ideas to control his conduct, he will, we have a right to expect, change suddenly from total failure to differentiate the signals to total success. He will or won't have the ideas, and will behave accordingly." ['01, p. 20.]

This same criterion of suddenness of change has been often used since then, notably by Yerkes and Köhler in their studies of the learning of the higher apes. It is admirably simple and objective, usable without acrimony by both the most confirmed introspectionist and the most rabid behaviorist.

There are other useful criteria, notably the nature of the response. If the response is one which does not occur in the animal's repertory of instincts or habits, but has to be fabricated by combining several elements from these or by modifying one or more elements, and if this fabrication occurs by way of some inner rehearsal or construction, the use of ideas is involved.

I shall treat of the evolution of such learning in a later lecture. Our present concern is with its nature and the principles that govern its action. We are especially concerned to discover how it is related to the principles of use, effect, identifiability of situation, availability of response, piecemeal activity, coöperative activity, and mental set, and whether it involves principles and powers beyond and above these.

(1) Learning by ideas is characterized by analysis. Gross total situations are replaced in thought by their elements.

Subtle and hidden qualities are picked out for emphasis. The bone which to the dog's mind is a gross total thing to be desired, seized, and gnawed may be to the man's mind a six-inch thing, a calcium-compound thing, a horizontal line, a vertical line, a weapon, a lever, a weight, or a reminder of human mortality.

(2) Learning by ideas is, as the name implies, characterized by the frequent presence of ideas as situations or as responses or as both. Whereas the bulk of the learning which dogs and cats and chicks and rats display consists of connections leading from external or perceptual situations straight to bodily acts or to impulsive tendencies closely attached to such acts, the insight learning of man operates with the aid of ideas which are free from narrow confinements.

(3) Some of these ideas may be very abstract and subtle. Such, for example, are the cardinal numbers two, three, four, five, etc., the ideas of position or sequence such as are attached to the words *in, on, up, down, above, below, before, after, long, short, quick, slow, again.*

(4) Some of these ideas have general meaning or reference.

(5) Often they are arranged in series forming an inner rehearsal or planning.

(6) Learning by ideas is also often characterized by selection—selection of elements within the situation to be active or prepotent and selection of one from several possible responses.

We have then to investigate the psychology of analysis, of abstract and general ideas, of inner planning, and of selection.

Analysis becomes obvious in the so-called "higher" forms of learning, but really almost all learning is analytic. A previous lecture noted piecemeal activity and differential emphasis as common features of the action of a situation. Connections very rarely, if ever, lead from an entire situation acting with equal efficacy of all its parts. Within any connection there are likely to be minor connections from parts of the situations to parts of the responses. Any part of the situation may contract not only a link or bond with the response as a whole but in addition a preferential bond or connection with some part thereof. When such a part of a situation happens alone or in a different context, it tends to evoke the total response that was previously bound to it and its previous context. It also tends to evoke especially that part of the previous response to which the preferential connection leads. If this preferential bond is strong, it may be the dominant determiner of the response to a situation composed of the old element or part plus a new context. A man forms an enormous number of bonds with elements of situations, some of them very subtle and abstract elements. His intellectual life consists in analyzing, abstracting or taking apart so as to get these elements in identifiable, usable form as truly as in forming connections with them after he gets them. In school, for example, the learning of language, reading, arithmetic, grammar, and science consists very largely of operations undertaken to disengage aspects, relations, and abstract qualities from the gross total things and events in which they are hidden.

These operations are relatively unsuccessful with exceedingly dull children. They seem on the surface unlike the operations used in learning ordinary habits. Historically, abstraction has been set apart as a higher and more logical activity than association. Consequently one is tempted to posit some new and special power of analysis to set these elements free from gross total situations or enable them to be recognized within such situations.

No such special power is needed. An examination of what happens in such cases, following the lead given by James in his law of discrimination by varying concomitants, provides a much more probable explanation. An element is elevated into independence of any context by appearing in many, each time with one same preferential connection, the rest of the response varying with the element's varying contexts.

Consider what we actually do to bring about the abstraction of an element. We use three means, attention to the element, varying concomitants, and comparison or contrast. In each of these three, it is connections that cause the analysis. We disconnect an element from, or elevate it above inert submergence in, a gross total by nothing more nor less than the ordinary process of connecting, operating by the laws of use and effect.

For example, suppose that the quality or element to be abstracted is sixness. We display some group of six, say, six boys, and direct attention to the how-manyness by such directions as: "How many boys are standing here? Are there more than four? Jack and Fred make two. Tom makes three. Dick makes four. Henry makes five. Bob makes six. There are six boys standing." "How many pencils are there here? (showing five.) Now I take one more. Five and one make six."

We have the learner respond to many situations each containing sixness but with varying concomitants, choosing the situations so as to encourage total responses each consisting of two parts, one always the same to form a preferential bond with the sixness, the other always a different one to form preferential bonds with the varying concomitants. For example, we form connections like these:

The sight of six boys and the thought *How many are there?* → *There are six boys.*

The sight of : : : and the thought *How many dots are there?* → *There are six dots.*

The sight of a line made from six inches |—|—|—|—|—|—| and the thought *How many inches long is the line?* → *It is six inches long.*

Hearing six taps and counting 1, 2, 3, 4, 5, 6, as one hears them, and the thought *How many are there?* → *There were six taps.*

In a dozen such we shall have twelve occurrences of sixness connected with six and only one occurrence each connecting it with boys or dots or length or taps, etc.

We may arrange for situations where the concomitants are not only varied but contrasting or opposite, as by using six girls after six boys, or six feet after six inches. By *contrasting* or *opposite* we mean that the elements of the responses which have preferential bonds with the two contrasting elements of the two situations are in large measure incapable of being made at the same time. If we had five such pairs, the connections formed would be as follows:

$$Sixness + a \rightarrow Six + A$$
$$Sixness + opp. \text{ of } a \rightarrow Six + (-A)$$
$$Sixness + b \rightarrow Six + B$$
$$Sixness + opp. \text{ of } b \rightarrow Six + (-B)$$
$$Sixness + c \rightarrow Six + C$$
$$Sixness + opp. \text{ of } c \rightarrow Six + (-C)$$
$$Etc.$$

The total result would be for sixness to be connected with six ten times and once each with A and $-A$, B and $-B$, C and $-C$, D and $-D$, and E and $-E$. These latter tendencies counterbalance each other in the sense that the pupil will not say or think *boys — girls* or *inches — feet* or *black — white* or *long — short*. The tendency for sixness to be associated with six is thus strengthened both by its own frequency and by the diminished competition from responses to the concomitants. We may also place the contrast between the element itself and its opposite. We may also use the two sorts of contrast together. The connections in the last case may be represented as follows:—

$$a + b \rightarrow r_1 + r_2$$
$$\text{opp. of } a + b \rightarrow r_{not\ 1} + r_2$$
$$a + \text{opp. of } b \rightarrow r_1 + r_{not\ 2}$$
$$\text{opp. of } a + \text{opp of } b \rightarrow r_{not\ 1} + r_{not\ 2}$$
$$a + c \rightarrow r_1 + r_3$$
$$\text{opp. of } a + c \rightarrow r_{not\ 1} + r_3$$
$$a + \text{opp. of } c \rightarrow r_1 + r_{not\ 3}$$
$$\text{opp. of } a + \text{opp. of } c \rightarrow r_{not\ 1} + r_{not\ 3}$$
$$\text{etc.}$$

Thus, the connections, leading from a to r_1 are strengthened; those from a to r_2 and $r_{not\ 2}$, and r_3 and $r_{not\ 3}$, etc. are mutually destructive. The connections from b, c, etc. to r_1 are offset by connections from b, c, etc. to $r_{not\ 1}$.

We use comparison by having the learner respond appropriately to four boys, five boys, six boys; four pencils, five pencils, six pencils; four hats, five hats, six hats; a bell rung four times, five times, six times; a command to clap hands four times, five times, six times, etc., etc.

From time to time during and after these connections are being formed, we test him with the element of sixness in new contexts and reward his successful responses, until he can discern sixness anywhere that it is necessary for him to do so.

In all this there is nothing beyond or above connection-forming. Elements are made to stand out in relief and arouse response irrespective of their context by the action of use, effect, piecemeal activity, and preferential connections. The force at work is not some transcendental faculty of analysis or insight or abstraction, but a tendency of situations to act piecemeal and a multitude of connections so marshaled as to strengthen the connection leading from an element to some preferential response and to weaken all other connections leading from it.

This process of analysis provides man with the abstract ideas which figure so largely in the so-called "higher" forms of learning. It also gives him ability to appreciate and use the subtle relations. Cause, effect, superiority, inferiority, co-ordination, subordination, and the like are disengaged from *related pairs* by the same action of many connections that disengages sixness, heat, or length from things. We learn the meaning of *and, if, though, because,* and *unless* by these same processes of attentive consideration, preferential bonds, varying concomitants, comparison, and contrast.

The process in the development of so-called concepts or general ideas is different, but the fundamental forces are much the same. From the dynamic point of view, a concept (such as *man, dog, square, circle, triangle, house, chair,* or *number*) is a thing to identify and classify by. Good concepts are ones that enable a person to classify things or events without mistakes. He acquires them by hearing the word or other symbol for the class in question connected either with many representative samples of the things or events which belong in that class, or with a statement of the combination of characteristics which entitles a thing or event to membership in that class. In the first method the efficacy of a multitude of connections with things or events alike in the possession of a certain combination of characteristics and differing in non-essentials is apparent. In the second method, the characteristics themselves have been made identifiable and available by analysis. In both methods the development of concepts is aided by the piecemeal activity of situations whereby a thing or event acts less as a gross undifferentiated unit and more as a total containing elements.

The psychology of inner rehearsal or planning with ideas is like that of external rehearsal or planning with objects, save that the content is thought in the one case and action in the other. One idea evokes another because it has been bound to it by the frequency or the after-effects of the connection. The principles of identifiability of the first term or situation, availability of the second term or response, trial, and system apply just as elsewhere. Especially important is the fact of trial—that the connection is often between the presence of one idea (say of $\frac{928}{16}$) and the demand for a certain other idea (say the quotient of $\frac{928}{16}$), which in turn evokes various trial procedures until the demand is satisfied. Thus past habits and trial with selection coöperate in our trains of thought as they do in our trains of action.

It has been customary for psychologists to contrast the acquisition of skill, habit formation, association, and memory with learning by selective and purposive thinking. In the former, it is said, the situation determines the response with little interference by the man's temporary mind set or permanent dispositions; the connections lead from concrete things or events as they are; and the laws of exercise and effect account for all that happens. In the latter there is selection or control or reasoning; the man selects from each situation to suit his interests, the connections lead from such features of it as he chooses, these connections are checked or facilitated, and the laws of connection-forming are inadequate to explain the course of thought.

There is much truth and utility in such a contrast, but it

is erroneous in two respects. It is unwise to assert that there is little interference or control by the mind's set or disposition in even the most associative learning, and it is false to assert that the laws of connection-forming are inadequate to explain the dynamics of even the most selective and purposive thinking.

As was stated in the last lecture, all learning is dependent upon the status of the learner. Even when an animal seems most subservient to the external situation, his inherited nature and past experiences coöperate with it to determine response.

The question of the adequacy of the laws of habit formation in explaining selective thinking will recur in a later lecture. For the present we may note two facts. First, selection is the rule rather than the exception in learning even in the learning of the lower animals. A hungry chick put in a pen, with food and companions visible outside, selects from the total congeries of sensory stimuli which are within the range of its receptors, letting some have much weight on its behavior and others little. When it jumps at the wall several times and fails to surmount it, the consequence acts to favor rejection of that tendency, and similarly, every step in its responses to the situation represents one thing done of many that might have been done, the one thing occurring never by chance in the strict sense, but as a true selection by the general nature and temporary set of the chick's mind.

Second, the satisfying or annoying consequences of connections are genuine selective forces in even the most subtle, involved, and rational learning of man. Whether or not they need assistance or direction by more recondite and more rational forces, we will not now investigate. At all events they are real and important. Whatever else it may be, thought is a series of varied reactions. As the series occurs, one or another response is selected, emphasized, and allowed to determine the next thought, because it relieves some annoying irritation or lack or satisfies some craving in the thinker. Certain responses are disregarded or discarded as useless or harmful because they fail to satisfy or because they produce actual discomfort. These annoyances and satisfactions are no less real because they lack the sensuous or emotional qualities of electric shock, food, fear, or social approval. To be thwarted in solving a problem in arithmetic is as truly annoying as to be thwarted in getting out of a box to food and companions.

They are no less real because they are less obvious to casual inspection, being often short-lived and symbolic. They live long enough to do their work; a tenth of a second of annoyance may lead a man to redirect his train of thought. A symbolic satisfier in the form of an inner "O. K.," like the "Rights" in our experiments, may be amply sufficient to validate and encourage a certain line of thought. The general diffuse excitement which accompanies some of the coarser satisfiers and annoyers is probably largely irrelevant for learning. It seems to be chiefly a sign that the body is being prepared for action, especially for violent muscular exertion. It is not the puffing of the steam or the blowing of the whistle that gives an engine its power.

Lecture 10

THINKING AND REASONING

IN much of human behavior, especially in purposive thinking and problem-solving, there is coöperative action of
many connections. Under the guidance of some mental set,
many tendencies start working; some of the responses produced thereby are discarded altogether; some are put aside
to be given influence later; some are used together to determine the next step.

The best way for us to realize the nature of this co-
operative action will be to study its products in some representative case. The case which I have chosen is the understanding of connected discourse, sentences and paragraphs.

In the hearing or reading of a paragraph, the connections
from the words singly and from various phrases somehow
coöperate to give certain total meanings. If some questions
about the paragraph are answered, the answers provide
useful material for studying the coöperation and organization of these connections. Consider for example the responses
made by 200 pupils in grade 6 to the following paragraph
and question:

J.

Read this and then write the answers to 1, 2, 3, 4, 5, 6,
and 7. Read it again as often as you need to.

In Franklin, attendance upon school is required of every
child between the ages of seven and fourteen on every day
when school is in session unless the child is so ill as to be unable to go to school, or some person in his house is ill with a
contagious disease, or the roads are impassable.

1. What is the general topic of the paragraph?

....

	Per cents	Number per thousand
J 1. Unanswered	18	180
Franklin	4½	45
In Franklin	1	10
Franklin attendance	1	10
Franklin School	1½	15
Franklin attending school	1	10
Days of Franklin	½	5
School days of Franklin	½	5
Doings at Franklin	1	10
Pupils in Franklin	½	5
Franklin attends to his school	½	5
It is about a boy going to Franklin	½	5
It was a great inventor	½	5
Because it's a great invention	½	5
The attendance of the children	½	5
The attendance in Franklin	½	5
School	7½	75
To tell about school	½	5
About school	4	40
What the school did when the boy was ill	½	5
What the child should take	½	5
If the child is ill	2	20
How old a child should be	½	5
If the child is sick or contagious disease	½	5
Illness	1	10
On diseases	½	5
Very ill	3	30
An excuse	2	20
The roads are impassable	1	10
Even rods are impossible	½	5
A few sentences	½	5
Made of complete sentences	½	5
A sentence that made sense	½	5

	Per cents	Number per thousand
A group of sentences making sense	½	5
A group of sentences	3	30
Subject and predicate	½	5
Subject	½	5
The sentence	½	5
A letter	½	5
Capital	5½	55
A capital letter	½	5
To begin with a capital	2	20
The first word	½	5
A general topic	½	5
Good topic	½	5
Leave half an inch space	2½	25
The heading	½	5
Period	½	5
An inch and a half	½	5
An inch and a half capital letter	½	5
The topic is civics	½	5
The answer	½	5

In this and in all similar tests of reading, the responses do not fall into a few sharply separate groups, but display a variety that seems likely to baffle explanation. A similar variety appears among the responses of pupils in grades 5 and 6 who read the following paragraph and questions:

I

Read this and then write the answers to 1, 2, 3, 4, and 5. Read it again as often as you need to.

Nearly fifteen thousand of the city's workers joined in the parade on September seventh, and passed before two hundred thousand cheering spectators. There were workers of both sexes in the parade, though the men far outnumbered the women.

1. What is said about the number of persons who marched in the parade? ....

2. Which sex was in the majority?

. . . .

3. What did the people who looked at the parade do when it passed by? . . . .

4. How many people saw the parade?

. . . .

5. On what date did the event described in the paragraph occur? . . . .

Answers to Question 1

Two hundred people
Three thousand
Thousand
Eighteen thousand
Two thousand
Five thousand
Ninety thousand
Twenty-five thousand
About thirty-five thousand
Nearly twenty thousand
More than ten thousand
There were about 25000
200,000
It was 200,000
About two thousand
Maybe No. 12
About 2700
Two hundred thousand spectators workers in the parade
Two hundred thousand spectators
Two hundred cheering
Nearly 115000 on Sept. of people
Nearly sixteen thousand
Hundred thousand spectators
It is said about the number or group of people
It is said that they are great
A very great deal

A lot of people
Congregation
There were a great lot of men
The men outnumbered the women
The men were more than the women
There were more men
They outnumbered the women
There the par on number the
The men were far ahead of the women
Men and woman
Citizens
They were workers
There were workers of both sexes
Workmen in the parade
Of all the working men
That the city workers joined the parade
Workers joined the parade
That they rejoin in the parade
They were joined
A number of workers joined the parade
Joined the parade
Workers join

They joined

They pass two hundred spectators

Before the spectators

Passed before two hundred thousand spectators

They two hundred thousand cheering spectators

Passed before 200000 and 15000

They passed nearly 5000

Passed before two hundred spectators

They marched before cheering spectators

Three thousand cheering them

People of both sexes cheering them

They are cheered

Parade before two hundred spectators

Parade spectators

They marched nice

They marched very nice

They kept in step

They marched very straight

They did good or bad

They look so nice

They clap their hands when they see the American flag

They keep their step and many others

There character

Honorable and good

The people said the parade large

Most of them were old

They are soldiers and marched

They say halt

The captain says march

There was a lot of floats

The people are killed by the war

The meddles

September seventh

Irish

The clue to the mystery is in the principle of potency or weight. Most of these responses are due to the over-potency or under-potency of certain of the connections with words or phrases in the paragraph or question. Some are due to wrong connections, that is, wrong meanings for words. Some are due to failure to examine the coöperating responses as they occur and failure to welcome or reject them according as they satisfy the mental set for the sake of which the reading was done. Some are due to right elements being put in wrong relations. But a large percentage, probably the majority of them, are due in whole or in part to the improper attachment of weight to connections and responses which are intrinsically good.

Consider first the over-potency of elements in the question. The first question about paragraph J was, "What is the general topic of the paragraph?" Over-potency of *paragraph* is shown by these responses:

A few sentences	Subject
Made of complete sentences	The sentence
A sentence that made sense	A letter
A group of sentences	Capital
Subject and predicate	A capital letter

When the *top-* of *topic* and *paragraph* are both over-potent, we have such responses as "Leave a half-inch space," "An inch and a half," "An inch and a half capital letter," and "The topic of paragraph is one inch in."

The second question about paragraph J was: "On what day would a ten-year-old girl not be expected to attend school?"

We find over-potency of *day* shown by "Monday," "Wednesday," and "Friday"; of *ten-year-old girl* in "The ten-year-old girl will be 5A."

Ten-year-old is over-potent in an interesting way, namely, in the very large number of responses of "On her birthday." Over-potency of *attend school* seems to be one part of the causation of "To attendance with Franklin," "Ever morning at half past 8," "She should," and "Because he did learn."

Consider next over- and under-potency of the words or phrases in the paragraph. The following list of responses shows that each of ten words taken from the paragraph is over-potent so as to appear clearly influential in the response to each of the first three questions (and in seven of the cases to the fourth question as well). These occur within 500 responses made by children in grades 5 to 8. Cases of under-potency would be still easier to collect.

The questions were as follows:

1. What is the general topic of the paragraph?
2. On what day would a ten-year-old girl not be expected to attend school?
3. Between what years is attendance upon school compulsory in Franklin?
4. How many causes are stated which make absence excusable?

(The numbers refer to the question to which the words were the response.)

Franklin   1. Franklin. 1. Franklin and the diseases. 1. Franklin topic.
2. Franklin.
3. Because it is a small city. 3. Franklin was in school 141 years.

attendance 1. Attendance.
2. To attendance with Franklin.
3. In Franklin attendance upon school is required. 3. Attending school 130 days.

school   1. School. 1. They must know their lessons.
2. In the beginning of school.
3. School in session. 3. In the years of school.

seven   1. Seven and fourteen. 1. How old a child should be.
2. He should attend school at 7 years. 2. Between seven and fourteen.
3. Seven years.
4. Under seven.

fourteen   1. Every child between seven and fourteen. 1. In Franklin how old they are.
2. Fourteen of every day. 2. Fourteen years.
3. Fourteen years. 3. Fourteen.
4. 7 to 14.

every   1. Every child.
2. Expected every day. 2. On every day.
3. Every year. 3. Every child between fourteen or thirteen.
4. Every day.

ill
1. Illness. 1. Very ill. 1. If the child is ill.
2. Ill. 2. A very bad throat.
3. He cannot go to school unless ill.
4. When child is ill. 4. Must be sick.

contagious
1. Contagious disease.
2. If she is sick or has a contagious disease.
3. Contagious disease.
4. Contagious disease.

disease
1. Fever. 1. About disease.
2. Often sick.
3. Unless ill or contagious disease. 3. Disease.
4. A terrible disease going out. 4. Because when a boy has disease.

impassable
1. The roads are impassable. 1. Snow.
2. When roads are impassable.
3. Seven to fourteen years or the roads are impassable.
4. Or the roads are impassable.

Any element of the situation may also have far *less* potency than it should. The following are cases from the responses of pupils in grades 5 to 8 to questions 1 to 5 on paragraph I.

Question 1

nearly—(Failure to include this in the response to 1 is of course very, very common.)

fifteen—"Thousand"

what is said about the—"Honorable and good," "They march very nice," "They marched very straight," "They did good or bad," and many similar responses.

number of persons—"They were workers," "Men and women," "That they rejoin in the parade," "Passed before cheering spectators."

who marched in the parade—The many responses of "200000," "They cheered them," etc.

All of question 1 except *parade* is under-potent—"There were a lot of floats."

Question 2

which—"Both sexes was in the parade," "There were both sexes there," "Workers of both sexes," "Men and women," "Two sexes," "Two of them."

sex—"City workers," "City workers of N. Y.," "The chief commander of all," "Working," "The front ones," "Spectators," "Cheering," "Fifteen thousand."

in the majority—"Women," "Sex outnumbered of women."

which . . . was in the majority—"The sex spectators," "Sexes," "In the parade," "Sexes in the parade," "There were men of other sex in the parade."

Question 3

what did the . . .do—"They were cheered by the people," "Two hundred."

people—"Tip his hat."

people who looked at—"Passed before two hundred," "Passed before a number of cheering spectators."

when it passed by—"Two hundred thousand cheering spectators passed."

it—"They saluted them," "They cheered them."

cheering—"Inspected the parade," "They were glad to see it," "They talked about it" (and many others).

All save *parade* underpotent—"September seventh," "Seventh Avenue."

Question 4

saw the parade—"The men outnumbered the women," "Far outnumbered."

two—"About 100000," "One hundred thousand," "Three hundred thousand."

hundred—"Two thousand."

thousand—"Two hundred."

two hundred [thousand]—"Fifteen thousand," "Nearly fifteen thousand," "Over 25000," "Over five hundred," "About 10000," "About 5000," "About 1000."

Question 5

what date—"There were workers of both sexes in the parade," "Thought the man fat out," "Described," "Sexes of the parade," "The parade," "And outnumbered women."

event described in paragraph—"March 4, 1915," "March 17," "April 23, 1903," "November 4," "December 4," "On Friday," "March 17," "March 18," "St. Patrick's day," "On the twenty-second of February," "St. Pattac," "1492," "1776," "1820."

Seventh—"September seventeenth" (a common error, often due to misperception or memory, probably), "September."

Sometimes the correct weighting of elements or factors is the simple one of choosing the right or essential element, that is, of letting one element have full potency and reducing the potencies of all others to zero. We then have the case of reasoning well known from William James's classic description.*

"It contains analysis and abstraction. Whereas the merely empirical thinker stares at a fact in its entirety, and remains helpless, or gets 'stuck,' if it suggests no concomitant or similar, the reasoner breaks it up and notices some one of its separate attributes. This attribute he takes to be the essential part of the whole fact before him. This attribute has properties or consequences which the fact until then was not known to have, but which, now that it is noticed to contain the attribute, it must have.

"Call the fact or concrete datum S;
the essential attribute M;
The attribute's property P.

"Then the reasoned inference of P from S cannot be made without M's intermediation. . . . *For his original concrete S the reasoner substitutes its abstract property, M.* What is true of M, what is coupled with M, then holds true of S, is coupled with S. As M is properly one of the *parts* of the

* James, *Principles of Psychology* (Henry Holt and Company).

entire S, *reasoning may then be very well defined as the substitution of parts and their implications or consequences for wholes*. And the art of the reasoner will consist of two stages:

"First, *sagacity*, or the ability to discover what part, M, lies embedded in the whole S which is before him;

"Second, *learning*, or the ability to recall promptly M's consequences, concomitants, or implications." ['93, Vol. 2, p. 330.]

Again on pages 357 and 362 of the *Briefer Course*, James writes:

"The essence of a thing is that one of its properties which is so *important for my interests* that in comparison with it I may neglect the rest. Amongst those other things which have this important property I class it, after this property I name it, as a thing endowed with this property I conceive it; and whilst so classing, naming, and conceiving it, all other truth about it becomes to me as naught. . . .

"Reasoning is always to attain some particular conclusion, or to gratify some special curiosity. It not only breaks up the datum placed before it and conceives it abstractly, it must conceive it *rightly* too; and conceiving it rightly means conceiving it by that one particular abstract character which leads to the one sort of conclusion which it is the reasoner's temporary interest to attain. . . .

"*Sagacity.* To reason, then, we must be able to extract characters,—not *any* characters, but the right characters for our conclusion. If we extract the wrong character, it will not lead to that conclusion." *

This selection of one element to have full weight and reduction of the weights of all else to zero is more truly regarded, not as the general rule of reasoning, but as a limiting and special case.

The general rule is that right thinking requires that proper potency be given to each element of the situation, and that thinking may be wrong or inadequate not only by failure to

* James, *Psychology—Briefer Course* (Henry Holt and Company).

pick the essential element of the situation, but also, and more often, by the attachment of too much or too little weight to any element or feature of it.

The next important feature of thinking things together is putting them in the proper relations. Each may be given due weight and may call up suitable associates, but thought will go wrong if the relations are confused. In the comprehension of paragraphs we have such cases as the following:

The paragraph was:

"You need a coal range for kitchen warmth and continuous hot-water supply, but in summer when you want a cool kitchen and less hot water, a gas range is better. The xyz ovens are safe. In the end ovens there is an extra set of burners for broiling."

The question was:

"What effect has the use of a gas range instead of a coal range upon the temperature of the kitchen?"

The answer was:

"A cool kitchen is used for a gas range."

In thinking about objects whose properties are familiar, such absurdities due to misplaced relations are usually prevented or remedied by the ideas of impossibility or undesirability which they call up. But in thinking with symbols or with unfamiliar content they are common.

Consider the following problem:

A, who now has five dollars less than B had before C gave B three times what B had already, will have half of a half of a half as much as B had after C made the gift to B, if C gives A two dollars. How much has A now?

If a thousand pupils in grade 7 or 8 are required to present some solution to this, their responses will probably include a score of combinations of relations besides those which are correct. C will appear as a recipient instead of a donor; gifts to A will be awarded to B or vice versa; halves of something will be added; five dollars will be subtracted from the credit of A; and still queerer shifts of five, three, two, and one half will be made.

As thinking progresses, each of its constituent responses is subject to certification or validation. If it passes muster in the judgment of the general set of mind in whose service the thinking is done, it is itself given weight in the determination of further responses. Or it may be rejected, or amended in this or that particular. Thinking may be wrong or inadequate because this process of validation is too easy-going to detect and correct the mistakes made in attaching weight to elements, putting them in relation, and having them evoke right associates.

A person who considers an intellectual problem and gets an answer or solution for it is beset by tendencies of literally every element in the problem to assume undue potency, to become dislocated from its proper relations, and to call up its own associations with too little regard for the general mental set or adjustment. If the person does get the right solution, that means that an elaborate hierarchy of connections is in operation and that a very delicate balance of power is maintained. Most, if not all, of the tendencies which produced the errors of our illustrations existed also in the pupils who made no such errors. The tendencies were there, but were prevented from determining final response by other competing and coöperating tendencies.

The compositions of forces which determine the direction of thought are thus highly elaborate and complex; but the forces themselves are very simple, being the elements in the situation and the connections leading from those elements and various combinations thereof which the past experience and present adjustment of the thinker provide.

The simple facts of over-potency and under-potency, dislocation of elements into wrong relations, and imperfect or erroneous associations are all that are needed to explain errors in thinking. Conversely, the right weighting of elements, held in the right relations, and connected with the right associates, explains correct thinking. Thinking and reasoning are very different from automatism, custom, and habit in their superficial appearance, and also in their power. But in their fundamental nature they are not the opposites of automatism, custom, and habit, but rather are bone of their bone and flesh of their flesh. They show the action of the simple general laws of connecting in cases where the connections are with elements of the situation rather than with gross totals, and where the connections compete and coöperate in subtle and complicated organizations. The inspection and validation whereby each succeeding step is welcomed or amended or discarded consist of situation-response connections in which the responses are cherishing, repeating, denying, and the like.

I conclude therefore that the general laws of human behavior which explain how a child learns to talk or dress himself and why he gets up in the morning and goes to bed at night also explain how he learns geometry or philosophy and why he succeeds or fails in the most abstruse problems, and that there exists no fundamental physiological contrast between fixed habits and reasoning.

But I conclude also that the complexity and subtlety of the competition and coöperation of connections required to understand, say, a page of a textbook in physics or a chapter of one of St. Paul's epistles, wherein each connection is given a certain potency and acts in certain relations to the others, is far beyond any description hitherto given by associationist psychology. The number of neurone connections which have to exist in order to create understanding of even one ordinary sentence such as, "If John and Mary come to your house before dinner, bring them to the pond," may well be over 100,000; and over a thousand of them or their derivatives may have to be active during the few seconds in which the sentence is heard and understood.

Lecture 11

THE EVOLUTION OF LEARNING IN GENERAL

THE same change in an animal may occur as a feature of learning or in other ways. The animal who once bit at a certain object may now neglect it, because he has learned to neglect it, or because he has outgrown the taste for it, or because he is not now hungry, or because his muscles are unready to contract. Learning is a form of change, distinguished from the changes of mere inner growth by being related to special external situations and usually by being much more rapid, and distinguished from adaptation, fatigue, excitability, depression, and other physiological shifts by being much more permanent.

In their simple and early stages the changes in animals which we call learning are hard to distinguish from changes which we call adaptation or fatigue. Indeed if an animal in which we cannot separate off sense-organs, muscles, and the like is gently touched once per minute and then reacts less and less to these touches, but the next hour or day is just as before, we may equally well say that he becomes adapted, or gets fatigued, or learns not to mind it for the time being. How the changes called learning evolved from the more general modifiability of living matter, we do not know. It is a fascinating subject for investigation in comparative physiology and psychology in the future.

We shall begin the story of learning at the point where the animal is modified by certain experiences, not by mere inner growth, so that it responds to the same external situation in a way different from that in which it responded before those experiences, and also retains this modification in a different manner and for a longer time than can be accounted for by adaptation or fatigue or changes in excitability.

This occurred far back in animal history. The earthworm studied by Yerkes ['12] learned, as a result of being given an electric shock when it followed its original tendency to seek the dark, to turn toward the light. Snails, according to Piéron ['11a and '11b], that at first drew back their tentacles when a shadow fell upon them, stopped doing so after fewer and fewer trials as the experiment progressed. Symanski ['12] and Turner ['12] taught cockroaches to turn back from the edge of a dark spot and thus avoid an electric shock. Cockroaches have also learned to take the right path through simple mazes. The crab (*Carcinus*) and crayfish learn to choose the right path to get back to water. [Yerkes, '02; Yerkes and Huggins, '03.] All the vertebrates apparently have the ability to learn.

The general pattern and features of the learning are extraordinarily alike over almost the entire range. Molluscs and arthropods—fishes, amphibians, reptiles, birds, and mammals manifest fundamentally the same process of learning. What that process is may best be seen from two concrete instances, one from near the bottom of the vertebrates and one from near the top.

The little fish Fundulus, on being shut up in one end of a tank in the light behind a screen of wire netting with a hole at one point, turns toward the shaded end and swims until he bumps his nose against the screen. He then turns, swims along, turns toward the shaded end and swims until he bumps his nose again. This behavior continues until he turns so as to face the hole and swims through it to a resting place in the shade. After he has had sufficient time for enjoyment, he is gently pushed back behind the screen again.

He responds as before, but with, in general, fewer bumps and a quicker arrival at the opening. And so on for trial after trial, with fewer and fewer turns in the direction away from the hole, fewer and fewer bumps against the screen, and a quicker and quicker arrival at the hole, until the fish, as soon as he is put in the accustomed spot behind the screen, turns toward the end of the screen where the hole is, swims there, turns, and swims through.

A Cebus monkey was kept in a large cage. Into the cage was put a box the door of which was held closed by a wire fastened to a nail which was inserted in a hole in the top of the box. If the nail was pulled up out of the hole, the door could be pulled open. In this box was a piece of banana. The monkey, attracted by the new object, came down from the top of the cage and fussed over the box. He pulled at the wire, at the door, and at the bars in the front of the box. He pushed the box about and tipped it up and down. He played with the nail and finally pulled it out. When he happened to pull the door again, of course it opened. He reached in and got the food inside. It had taken him thirty-six minutes to get in. Another piece of food being put in and the door closed, the occurrences of the first trial were repeated, but there was less of the profitless pulling and tipping. He got in this time in two minutes and twenty seconds. With repeated trials the animal finally came to drop entirely the profitless acts and to take the nail out and open the door as soon as the box was put in his cage. He had, as we should say, learned to get in.

The process involved in these acts of learning is evidently a process of selection. The animal is confronted by a state of affairs or "situation." He reacts in the way that he is moved by his innate nature or previous training to do, by a number of acts. These acts include the particular act or series of acts that is appropriate, and he is rewarded. In later trials the connection leading to this one act or series of acts is more and more strengthened; this one act or series of acts is more and more closely associated with that situation. It is selected from amongst the others apparently by reason of the satisfaction to the animal which follows it. The less profitable acts occur less and less often as responses to that situation. Consequently, the animal finally performs in that situation only the one act or series of acts.

Here we have the most widespread sort of learning in the world. There need be no reasoning, no process of inference or comparison; there need be no thinking about things, no putting two and two together; there need be no ideas— the animal may not think of the box or of the food or of the act he is to perform. What we surely know is that he comes after the learning to do a certain thing in certain circumstances which before the learning he did not do in those same circumstances. Human beings are accustomed to think of intellect as the power of having and controlling ideas and of ability to learn as synonymous with ability to have ideas. But learning by having ideas is really one of the rare and isolated events in nature. The common form of intelligence of animals, their habitual method of learning, is not by the acquisition of ideas, but by the selection of responses.

Dogs and cats may have a few ideas, inner representations, of certain common objects often experienced and responded to in many diverse contexts, and of certain common acts often performed as responses to many diverse situations. They may thus in a certain sense think of "good food," "friendly smell," "turn back," "bite it," and the like. But they do not have many or use them very much. As a rule, they learn by trial and success, not by planning, or imitating, or being shown, or being put through an act.

The monkeys, our nearest relatives physically, and especially the chimpanzees, more often show signs of inner consideration of a situation and guidance in their learning by ideas about it. But even they learn in very large measure by the "try, try again" method, with gradual selection of a suitable response by the satisfaction it brings rather than by deliberation and insight.

Indeed this same type of learning is found in man. When we learn to drive a golf ball or play tennis or billiards, when we learn to tell the price of tea by tasting it or to produce a certain note exactly with the voice, we do not learn in the main by virtue of any ideas that are explained to us, or by any inferences that we reason out. We learn by the gradual selection of the appropriate act or judgment and its association with the circumstances or situation requiring it, in just the way that the animals do.

This purely associative learning by trial and success to respond in this, that, and the other way to situations directly presented to sense is the same in its general nature from the minnow to man, but great developments take place in the quantity and quality of the associations formed. If we follow the course of animal evolution, we find the associations thus made between situation and act growing in number, being formed more quickly, and becoming more complex and more delicate. The fish can learn to go to certain places, to take certain paths, to avoid certain enemies, to bite at certain objects and refuse others, but not much more. It is an arduous proceeding for him to learn to get out of a small pen by swimming up through a hole in a screen. The monkey can learn to do thousands of things. It is a comparatively short and easy task for him to learn to get into a box by unhooking a hook, pushing a bar around, and pulling out a plug. He learns quickly to climb down to a certain place when he sees a letter T on a card, and to stay still when he sees a K.

This growth in the number, speed of formation, delicacy, and complexity of associations possible for an animal reaches its acme in the case of man. Even if we leave out of question the power of reasoning, and the possession of a multitude of ideas and abstractions, man is still the intellectual leader of the animal kingdom by virtue of the superior development in him of the power of forming associations between situations or sense-impressions and acts—by virtue of the degree to which the mere learning by selection possessed by all intelligent animals has advanced.

So much of the evolution of human learning is clear and simple enough. Man forms direct connections of the animal sort between a sensed situation and an act in the animal way by frequency of connection and satisfyingness of after-effect, but he forms more of them, forms them with subtler elements of situations and in more complex series and includes in his acts a wide repertory of delicate and complex movements of manipulation, facial expression, and vocal sounds.

To this extraordinary development of the common animal type of learning, man adds the ability to acquire an enormous fund of ideas, the ability to review in thought what has happened and plan for what may happen, to analyze and conceive and infer. Concerning the evolution of these distinctively human abilities William James wrote in 1890, "The more sincerely one seeks to trace the actual course of psychogenesis, the steps by which as a race we may have come by the peculiar mental attributes which we possess, the more clearly one perceives 'the slowly gathering twilight close in utter dark.'"

In a certain sense that is still true. We do not know when *homo sapiens* split off from the parent anthropoid stock, whether for example he is uncle, cousin, or nephew of the chimpanzees. We may in the future find the skulls of missing links, but their behavior and learning we can never test. But forty years of study of animal and human learning have made James's metaphor at least inapplicable. Although mental evolution is far from clear, it is clearing up; we see more and more light. And I shall propose for your consideration a theory of the evolution of human intellect which has now much more evidence in its favor than when it was first brought forth.

This theory is that the rich supply of ideas, the insights and reasonings which seem to separate human learning so sharply from the great bulk of animal learning, are themselves secondary results of the tremendous increase in the number and fineness of the connections which the human animal can form. A quantitative difference in associative learning is by this theory the producer of the qualitative differences which we call powers of ideation, analysis, abstract and general notions, inference, and reasoning.

One merit of this theory is its agreement with what is known concerning the evolution of the associative neurones in the brain upon which intellect and learning depend. Man does not, so far as is known, have new varieties of neurones, or new modes of action of neurones, but he does have many more of them, with far greater possibilities of interconnection than exist in other animals.

A second merit of the theory is its agreement with the development of learning during the life history of the individual human being. The learning of the baby during its first twelve months or more is of the general animal type, connecting specific acts with directly sensed situations by frequency and after-effect. He has few ideas; he learns by trial rather than by insight. But from the age of six or eight months on he makes connections in enormous numbers. Each toy is held in scores of positions, and moved in scores of directions, and the eyes observe it again and again so that one rattle or spoon or block is seen in literally scores of aspects and hundreds of settings. Almost all objects whatsoever of suitable size are pushed along, pulled back, turned over, let fall, picked up, and the like, so that these movements enter into literally thousands of connections. The baby's babble includes, I think, more different articulate sounds than any language; and combinations of these, optimistically interpreted by the family members as real words or accepted as the baby's own language, become connected with valued after-effects. The speech of others is attended to by him and the words, phrases, and sentences heard are associated with the things and events which they go with. If a baby boy and a baby kitten, born on the same day, were kept together side by side for two years so that both heard just the same words on just the same occasions and if both could be given just the same treatment after each, on their second birthday the child would understand probably at least fifty times as many words, phrases, and sentences as the cat.

Within a year or two the baby that at twelve or fourteen months played like a kitten, only in many more ways, and chattered like a monkey, only with many more sounds and combinations of sounds, and learned like a puppy, only so many more acts and facts, comes to have ideas, think in words about qualities and relations, talk to himself, and plan. He makes inductions and deductions in distinctive human fashion. The product of his reasoning is often irrational because of faulty data, but the processes are all there.

I quote representative samples from a collection made many years ago by Brown:

(2 yrs.) T. pulled the hairs on his father's wrist. Father. "Don't, T. you hurt papa!" T. "It didn't hurt grandpa."

(2 yrs. 5 mos.) M. said, "Gracie can't walk, she wear little bits of shoes; if she had mine, she could walk. When I get some new ones, I'm going to give her these, so she can walk."

(2 yrs. 9 mos.) He usually has a nap in the forenoon, but Friday he did not seem sleepy, so his mother did not put him to bed. Before long he began to say, "Bolly's sleepy; mamma put in the crib!" This he said very pleasantly at first; but as she paid no attention to him, he said, "Bolly cry, then mamma will." And he sat down on the floor and roared.

(3 yrs.) It was between five and six in the afternoon; the mother was getting the baby asleep. J. had no one to play with. He kept saying, "I wish R. would come home; mamma, put baby to bed, so R. will come home." I usually get home about six, and as the baby is put to bed about half-past five, he had associated the one with the other.

(3 yrs.) W. likes to play with oil paints. Two days ago my father told W. he must not touch the paints any more, for he was too small. This morning W. said, "When my papa is a very old man, and when I am a big man and don't need any papa, then I can paint, can't I, mamma?"

(3 yrs.) G.'s aunt gave him ten cents. G. went out, but soon came back saying, "Mamma, we will soon be rich now." "Why so, G.?" "Because I planted my ten cents, and we will have lots of ten cents growing."

(2 yrs.) B. climbed into a large express wagon, and would not get out. I helped him out, and it was not a minute before he was back in the wagon. I said, "B., how are you going to get out of there now?" He replied, "I can stay here till it gets little and then I can get out by my own self."

(3 yrs.) F. is not allowed to go to the table to eat unless she has her face and hands washed and her hair combed. The other day she went to a lady visiting at her house and said, "Please wash my face and hands and comb my hair; I am very hungry."

(3 yrs.) If C. is told not to touch a certain thing, that it will bite him, he always asks if it has a mouth. The other day he was examining a plant, to see if it had a mouth. He was told not to break it, and he said, "Oh, it won't bite, because I can't find any mouth." ['92, *passim.*]*

* H. W. Brown, "Some Records of the Thoughts and Reasonings of Children," *The Pedagogical Seminary* (Clark University Press), II (1892), 358-396.

A third merit of this theory that a simple quantitative variation in the general animal sort of learning, paralleling a variation in the number of neurone connections, causes the appearance of what we call ideas, insights, reasoning, and the like, is its harmony with the facts about the differences amongst individual human beings in the degree of development of these so-called higher powers.

If these higher powers come in the race as a consequence of a great volume of particular associations, there ought to be in individual men a close correlation or correspondence between amount of knowledge on the one hand and degree of intellect on the other—between the number of facts a man knows and the quality of his reasoning. And there is. The person who has an enormous fund of information and skill should, other things being equal, be the good thinker. He is. Sagacity should go with erudition. It does.

Until recently the opposite doctrine was the accepted one, namely, that a man may know and do well hundreds of thousands of particular things and yet be very weak in reasoning—in analytic and selective and relational thinking. The standard orthodox view of the surface nature of intellect was that it was divided rather sharply into a lower half, mere connection-forming or the association of ideas, which acquired information and specialized habits of thinking, and a higher half characterized by abstraction, generalization, the perception and use of relations, the selection and control of habits in inference or reasoning, and ability to manage novel or original tasks. The orthodox view of its deeper nature, so far as it received attention, was that the mere connection-forming or association of ideas depends upon the physiological mechanism whereby a nerve stimulus is conducted to and excites action in neurones A B C rather than any others, but that the higher processes depend upon something quite different. There was little agreement as to what this some-

Look at the first word in line 1. Find the other word in the line which means the same or most nearly the same. Write its number on the line at the right side of the page. Do the same in lines 2, 3, 4, etc. Lines A, B, C and D show the way to do it. Do all the lines you can. Write only one number for each line.

A. beast . . . 1 afraid . . . 2 words . . . 3 large . . . 4 animal . . . 5 bird 4

B. baby . . . 1 cradle . . . 2 mother . . . 3 little child . . . 4 youth . . . 5 girl 3

C. raise . . . 1 lift up . . . 2 drag . . . 3 sun . . . 4 bread . . . 5 deluge 1

D. blind . . . 1 man . . . 2 cannot see . . . 3 game . . . 4 unhappy . . . 5 eyes 2

Begin:

1. await . . . 1 pace . . . 2 slow . . . 3 wait for . . . 4 tired . . . 5 quit ....

2. beautify . . . 1 make beautiful . . . 2 intrude . . . 3 exaggerate . . . 4 insure . . . 5 blessed ....

3. bug . . . 1 insect . . . 2 a vehicle . . . 3 fiber . . . 4 abuse . . . 5 din ....

4. arrange . . . 1 put in order . . . 2 hasten . . . 3 distance . . . 4 frighten . . . 5 charge ....

5. different . . . 1 not the same . . . 2 quarrelsome . . . 3 better . . . 4 complete . . . 5 not here ....

6. cotton . . . 1 cloth . . . 2 small bed . . . 3 hut . . . 4 flour . . . 5 herd ....

7. blacken . . . 1 a fern . . . 2 interpose . . . 3 impel . . . 4 make black . . . 5 slack ....

8. ablaze . . . 1 ostensible . . . 2 on fire . . . 3 slightly . . . 4 loaf about . . . 5 urbane ....

9. avenue . . . 1 justice . . . 2 arrival . . . 3 street . . . 4 jury . . . 5 library ....

10. bench . . . 1 tool . . . 2 pull ashore . . . 3 opinion . . . 4 seat . . . 5 pond ....

11. confess . . . 1 agree . . . 2 mend . . . 3 deny . . . 4 admit . . . 5 mingle ....

12.	backward	1 downwards . . . 2 after . . . 3 toward the rear . . . 4 defense . . . 5 arrears
13.	advertise	1 detain . . . 2 explore . . . 3 give notice of . . . 4 adverse . . . 5 newspaper
14.	combat	1 fight . . . 2 dismay . . . 3 club . . . 4 expedition . . . 5 comb
15.	blond	1 polite . . . 2 dishonest . . . 3 dauntless . . . 4 coy . . . 5 fair
16.	broaden	1 efface . . . 2 make level . . . 3 elapse . . . 4 embroider . . . 5 widen
17.	chubby	1 indolent . . . 2 obstinate . . . 3 irritable . . . 4 plump . . . 5 muscular
18.	concern	1 see clearly . . . 2 engage . . . 3 furnish . . . 4 disturb . . . 5 have to do with
19.	cargo	1 load . . . 2 small boat . . . 3 hem . . . 4 draught . . . 5 vehicle
20.	clutch	1 exploit . . . 2 nest . . . 3 flit . . . 4 grasp . . . 5 cane
21.	awe	1 lamb . . . 2 fear . . . 3 tool . . . 4 mound . . . 5 opera
22.	aged	1 years . . . 2 active . . . 3 old . . . 4 merciful . . . 5 punctual
23.	arrive	1 answer . . . 2 rival . . . 3 enter . . . 4 force . . . 5 come
24.	blunt	1 dull . . . 2 drowsy . . . 3 deaf . . . 4 doubtful . . . 5 ugly
25.	accustom	1 disappoint . . . 2 customary . . . 3 encounter . . . 4 get used . . . 5 business
26.	bade	1 gaze . . . 2 a tool . . . 3 fetched . . . 4 wait . . . 5 ordered
27.	bog	1 ebb . . . 2 disorder . . . 3 swamp . . . 4 field . . . 5 difficulty
28.	cascade	1 hat . . . 2 waterfall . . . 3 firmament . . . 4 disaster . . . 5 box
29.	bray	1 cry of an ass . . . 2 bowl . . . 3 cry of an ox . . . 4 frustrate . . . 5 raven's cry
30.	disembark	1 unearth . . . 2 go ashore . . . 3 dislodge . . . 4 disparage . . . 5 strip

thing was, indeed little effort to think or imagine what it could be, but there was much confidence that it was not the mechanism of habit-formation.

I became suspicious of this orthodox view years ago on general grounds. The suspicion was confirmed by experience with intelligence tests, such as, for example, the fact that very many of the Binet tests for the early ages are informational, and that a test of range of vocabulary pure and simple is an excellent intelligence test. So about four years ago, Dr. Tilton and I subjected the question to a crucial experiment as follows:

We prepared tests which were as exclusively informational and associational as we could make them, such as the tests of mere range of word knowledge and mere arithmetical information and computation shown in part below.

I. E. R. ARITHMETIC, ASSOC., I

Write or print your name here very clearly . . . .

Add:

a.	b.	c.	d.	e.	f.	g.
¾	⅕	6	7¼	5 hrs. 42 min.	5 ft. 8½ in.	2¾
¼	⅘	3⅜	6½	4 hrs. 28 min.	5 ft. 10¼ in.	4⁷⁄₁₂
¾	⅖	8¾	8⅜	4 hrs. 56 min.	6 ft. 1¼ in.	1½

Multiply:

h.	i.	j.	k.	l.
623	145	4 lb. 9 oz.	18	15¾
7	206	3	3⅔	8

Divide:

m.	n.	o.	p.
$60 \div 9 =$	$12 \overline{\smash{)}2.76}$	$¾ \div 5 =$	$9⅝ \div 3¾ =$

Write the answers to these questions:

    q. 1 pound is how many ounces?   _____

    r. 1 bushel is how many quarts?   _____

    s. 1 mile is how many feet?   _____

    t. What is the average of 9, 10, 11, 11 and 14?   _____

    u. What per cent of 80 is 24?   _____

    v. How much is 125% of 16?   _____

    w. 1 right angle is how many degrees?   _____

    x. 1 barrel of flour is how many pounds?   _____

    y. Write 18 in Roman numerals.   _____

    z. Write 1,000 in Roman numerals.   _____

    aa. What is the cube of 10?   _____

    bb. What is the square root of 25?   _____

We also prepared tests which were as full of relational and selective thinking as we could make them. Such were tests in completing sentences and answering questions which required rational comprehension of paragraphs, and tests in novel mathematical tasks, such as those shown below.

I. E. R. ARITHMETICAL COMPLETION, D 3

Write or print your name and age and the school grade you are in here very plainly.

Name......................... Age..... Grade.....

In the lines below, each number is gotten in a certain way from the numbers coming before it. Study out what this way is in each line, and then write in the space left for it the number that should come next. The first two lines are already filled in as they should be.

SAMPLES {	2,	4,	6,	8,	10,	..*12*..	
	11,	12,	14,	15,	17,	..*18*..	

			$\frac{1}{12}$	$\frac{1}{2}$	$1\frac{1}{12}$	$1\frac{1}{3}$	....
			$\frac{1}{25}$	$\frac{1}{5}$	1	5	....
	41	44	45	48	49	52	53	....
		12	16	22	26	32	36	....
		27	30	21	24	15	18	....
				91	$79\frac{3}{4}$	$68\frac{1}{2}$	$57\frac{1}{4}$	....
				$1\frac{3}{16}$	$1\frac{3}{8}$	$1\frac{9}{16}$	$1\frac{3}{4}$	....
7	11	15	16	20	24	25	29	....
		7	16	19	28	31	40	....
40	39	37	34	33	31	28	27	....

Write the numbers and signs in each line in the right order so that they make a true statement or equation. Line A has been done to show you what you are to do.

A.		3	3	6	=	+	Ans. $3 + 3 = 6$.
1.	5	6	30		=	×	
2.	8	11	88		=	÷	
3.	2	8	8	8	=	+	×
4.	$\frac{1}{2}$	10	16	80	=	×	÷

We may think and speak of these four sets of tests as language information, mathematical information, language reasoning, and mathematical reasoning. Dr. Tilton ['26] tested many individuals each with all four sets of tests.

The correspondence between an individual's score or ranking in language information and language reasoning is very close. So is the correspondence between rank in mathematical information and mathematical reasoning. They are nearly or quite as close as the correspondence between the two tests of information, or that between the two tests of reasoning. This holds true even though educational environment is roughly equalized by using children of the same school grade (the 8th) in the same school system. Quantity of associative learning and ability to deal with abstract qualities and relations, different though they may seem, are intimately related in mental dynamics and presumably depend upon a common cause.

Until some one presents a likelier theory, we may then work upon the hypothesis that human capacity to learn developed from the general mammalian and primate capacity by a quantitative extension.* And this may encourage us to believe in the possibility of the further evolution of human intellect and learning.

Along with the increase in capacity for forming connections there developed a wider and more diversified interest in having experiences, making movements, and being a cause (that is, doing something to make something happen) and in having ideas and playing with them. Here, as elsewhere, a certain normal use of an organ is a source of satisfaction.

---

* This extension was probably not equal in all directions. As we have already suggested, responses of facial expression and articulate sounds probably increased greatly, but responses of erecting the hair and moving the ears may have actually fallen off. The possibility of preferential connections with elements sensed by vision probably increased more than the possibility of connections with elements sensed by smell.

Having shown reason to believe that quantity of connections produced human thinking, our next duty is to show how it did so. In one sense I cannot do that at all. I cannot take you back to the time (perhaps millions of years ago) when man first had a human mind and had just begun to have ideas, to start language, and to use clubs or stones; and picture how his richer fund of connections gave birth to ideas. For we have no evidence to help us guess what these connections were, or what ideas he first acquired, or how rapidly man got his mind.

But in another sense a reasonable hypothesis can be made. We can justifiably conceive how in general a multitude of particular connections creates human thinking. These conceptions will follow lines parallel to those of the last two lectures, in which analysis, abstraction, general notions, and reasoning were shown to be derived from, and indeed constituted out of, connections.

The ball which to a cat is a thing to chase and strike at and worry is to a baby a thing to chase and strike at and poke and roll and try to get in the mouth and squeeze and drop and suck and throw and do many other things to. The bottle, which, to a dog would be a thing to smell at and paw, is to the child a thing to grab and suck and turn over and drop and pick up and pull at and finger and rub against his toes and so on. The sight of the bottle or of the ball thus becomes associated with many different reactions, and thus by our general law tends to gain a position independent of any of them, to evolve from the condition of being a portion of the cycles *see-grab, see-drop, see-turn-over,* etc., to the condition of being a definite idea.

The infant's vague feelings of total situations are by virtue of the detailed working of his brain all ready to split up into parts, and his general activity and curiosity provide the multitude of different connections which allow them to

do so. The dog, on the other hand, has few or no ideas because his brain acts in coarse fashion and because there are
few connections with each single process.

In the evolution of learning, the primates link man to the
general mammalian stock almost as surely as they do in
physical form. Monkeys, apes, chimpanzees, orang-utans,
and gorillas, although they differ appreciably among themselves in mental traits, all stand mentally between other
mammals and man. They learn more things than dogs or
cats or rats or horses. They show a more general curiosity
and love of experience for experience's sake. As a consequence according to our theory, or as an accompaniment in
any case, they present more evidence of ideas. First, they
more often shift suddenly from inability to complete success. Illustrations of this were given in a previous lecture.

In the second place, they are more moved by representative factors more or less equivalent to images or memories,
not mere sensed situations. Behavior in so-called delayed-
reaction experiments is one of the best tests of this.

Yerkes ['28b] put food in one of six cans distinguishable
by size, color, or markings, which were placed on a turn-
table. This turn-table was then rotated out of sight of the
gorilla who was the subject of the experiment so that, if the
animal chose the correct container after the interval, he
did so by having held in mind some sort of representation
of that particular container's appearance. The times varied
from a few seconds to ten minutes. The percentage of correct responses came to be about five times what chance could
have given.

A delayed response to the position of a food-container
appeared in Yerkes's chimpanzees after delays varying from
a few minutes up to three hours. Delayed responses to color
as an isolated factor were difficult to learn, but Yerkes is
convinced that the number of successful choices considered

in connection with the behavior of the animals before and after the choice shows that such delayed responses can be made after thirty minutes at least. He concludes "that the chimpanzee is capable of a form of delayed response hitherto known and experimentally demonstrated only in man" (and since found also in the gorilla). ['28a, p. 269.]

Other experiments with primates, especially Tinklepaugh's experiments with *Macacus rhesus* and *Macacus cynomologus,* also indicate that representative factors play a much larger rôle in the life of the primates than in that of mammals in general.

The exact degree to which the learning of the primates has advanced beyond that of the mammals in general toward that of man is, however, by no means clear. On the one hand, we have behavior such as that of Köhler's chimpanzee that joined two sticks together to make a long stick to get food with and such as the following from Yerkes's gorilla. "It was the morning of February 18. The night had been rainy and the cage was very wet. About the grill where Congo habitually sat or stood while manipulating the turntable to obtain her breakfast were puddles of water. When I summoned her to the day's work she emerged from her sleeping room somewhat unwillingly, looked about the cage, hesitated a few seconds as if undecided whether to approach the grill in obedience to my command or to refuse to work, and then turned about and reëntered the sleeping room. A moment later she came out, carrying in her arms a bundle of hay from her bed. Approaching the grill, she placed the hay on the wet ground immediately in front of it and seating herself comfortably upon the dry cushion thus provided, indicated her readiness to operate the turntable. A few times previously she had been seen to carry hay from the sleeping room into the cage and play with it or sit on it, but never had she been seen definitely to use hay at the grill or elsewhere to protect her from the cold or dampness of the sand-covered ground. Whether or not this act was an accompaniment or expression of insight, it certainly was most highly adaptive." ['28b, p. 53f.]

But such cases are very rare. They occur with a seven-year-old gorilla or chimpanzee perhaps one ten-thousandth as often as with a seven-year-old child. Much of their behavior shows the same restriction to direct connections with sensed situations that is characteristic of the lower mammals. Yerkes's gorilla, for example, having learned to remove a wound chain from one tree, failed to do so when it was wound around another tree. Having learned to stack boxes in a pile and climb on them to secure food hanging from one tree, she failed to do so when the food was hung from another tree. Only after special practice *ad hoc* did she come to do so.

If we think of association or habituation and reasoning or insight as separate powers, the behavior of the primates seems inconsistent. They should show the latter less or more than they do. But if we regard the latter as a product of a quantitative change in the former, the behavior is just what we should expect.

On the whole then we can see a clear and simple and easy course of mental evolution from the mind of a cat or mouse or rabbit that acquires a few thousand mental connections by muscular trial, error, and success, to the mind of a man who surveys the situation, analyzes it into its elements, enacts various programs in the symbols of thought, and selects the successful one by inner judgment of its worth. No new kind of brain tissue is needed, no new varieties of neurones are needed, nothing save a mere increase in the number of associative neurones. It might be no harder for whatever causes variations to produce this variation in some species of primate than to produce the differences in size and shape which distinguish the gorilla from the chimpanzee, or the orang-utan from the dog-faced ape.

Nowhere more truly than in his mental capacities is man a part of nature. His instincts, that is, his inborn tendencies to feel and act in certain ways, show throughout marks of kinship with the lower animals, especially with our nearest relatives physically, the primates. His sense-powers show no new creation. His intellect we have seen to be a simple though extended variation from the general animal sort. This again is presaged by the similar variation in the case of the primates. Amongst the minds of animals that of man leads, not as a demigod from another planet, but as a king from the same race.

Lecture 12

THE EVOLUTION OF LEARNING IN RECENT TIMES: FUTURE POSSIBILITIES

ACCORDING to the hypothesis which we considered in the previous lecture, there evolved, nobody knows just when or how, primates possessed of brains which could form an enormous number of connections, much greater than their relatives, the ancestors of the present anthropoids, could form. They also probably had a very extensive repertory of movements of the throat and mouth parts, and enjoyed prattling, gurgling, chortling, and squealing when they were babies much as we do. They also probably reacted to situations in a more piecemeal fashion than other primates did. Psychologically they were men. Whether they then had the opposable thumb, the bony and muscular structure for walking upright, and so forth as men as well as the brains of men, does not concern us.

They had the capacity to form enough more connections to set their learning apart from that of other primates. They could learn more things, and could learn to respond to subtler parts or elements of the objects and events of nature. They were variations which had the possibility of a rich life of ideas, including abstract and general notions, inner planning, and learning by deliberate analysis and selection.

If we accept this hypothesis, we naturally ask the question: What has been the .evolution of learning since then? How far does our learning differ from that of these men of, say, ten thousand generations ago?

Since the facts and speculations to which this question leads will be as appropriate to any other reasonable hypothesis about the origin of human faculty, we may profit by considering them even if we feel no confidence whatever in the hypothesis itself.

Strangely enough, we do not know whether the native ability or inborn capacity of man to learn is any greater now than it was a million years ago. The commonest opinion of biologists and anthropologists and psychologists would probably be that it is, but an expert minority might deny this. The Ayes would argue that since, in early days, man depended on his wits in his struggle for survival, the duller ones must oftener have died before producing offspring; and perhaps also that so great a difference as that between present human capacity and the learning of our non-human ancestors could not have occurred by one or two mutations in the remote past, but must have been built up in parts by a long series of such. This second argument is perhaps mistaken in assuming that the difference is so very great biologically. A tenfold, even a hundredfold, increase in the number of connections possible in the brain might be biologically as likely to occur as horns on the head or two stomachs. The magnitude of the variation itself need not be equal to the magnitude of its consequences.

The Noes would argue that within historic times the evidence of progressive gain in native capacity to learn is dubious, and that the use of better tools for learning and methods of learning and better content to be learned is adequate to account for any superiority of the present over the past, near or remote.

Psychology contributes one important set of facts to the discussion, which, however, leave the decision in nearly as much doubt as before. These facts concern the form of distribution and amount of variability in so-called general intelligence, which is probably a close indicator of ability to learn with ideas and symbols.

If we take all the white children aged eleven to twelve or thirteen attending public schools in a group of northern cities and test them with the National Intelligence Test or the Otis or the Haggerty, and correct the scores so as to eliminate the effects of inequalities in the units of scoring, we find the distribution to be as shown in Fig. 9. There is a

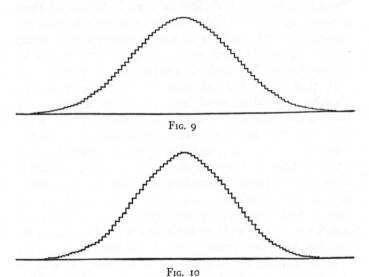

Fig. 9

Fig. 10

continuous variation up and down from mediocrity. There is a very wide range from the top to the bottom. Such measurements made in an hour or less are afflicted with a rather large chance error. But if this had been eliminated by using, say, the average of ten or twenty such tests, the continuity of the distribution would be just as certain as before. The range of variation would be somewhat decreased, approximately to the amount shown in Fig. 10.

If children of those cities so dull as to be excluded from school, but whose dullness was not due to any accident or disease or other specially untoward condition, were added to the group, the variations at the extreme low end would be increased in number, and some new ones at still lower points would be added. If children in school whose dullness was due to some accident, disease, shock, or the like were excluded from the group, there would be a few scattered losses, especially from the low extreme. If, besides all these precautions, only the children of the same environment (say, children brought up in a certain orphanage from birth) were used, the continuity would still be in force. The variability would be decreased still further, but not greatly.

If, that is, we had measures of the native intellectual capacity of children freed from disturbing environmental factors, the variations would be continuous up and down from one type, mediocrity, and would range from such a capacity, or such genes, as would result in, under the average conditions of American life, an I. Q. of 150 or higher down to such genes as would result under the same conditions in an I. Q. of 50 or less. After living twenty years in even a very favorable environment, a few of the latter would not be able to learn things much harder than to get into bed and cover oneself with the bedclothes, to open a door by turning an ordinary knob, or lifting a latch, to respond to a few directions like "Shake hands" by holding out one's hand.

The native intellectual capacity of man, the genes for intellect, vary from a status comparable to that of the genes of an average dog or cat to a status able to produce, even under rather unfavorable environments, Aristotles, Dantes, Newtons, Spinozas, Pasteurs, and Einsteins. The variation in product is continuous, which makes it highly probable that a fairly large number of genes, at least a half-dozen or more, are concerned. The number of genes may well be very much greater than that.

These facts are important because they indicate a possibility that the genes which are the heritable basis of intellect and ability to learn may have increased in number or in power since the time of man's origin, and are capable of further increase in the future. On the other hand, they cast doubt on the selection of the better learners for survival and parenthood. If the dull have been eliminated, we should not expect now to find men born with learning ability at or near the average level of the mammalia in general. But we do.

Changes in the inborn capacity to learn are hidden and doubtful, but changes in what is learned, and in the means and methods by which it is learned, are clear and certain, at least for the historical period of the life of the human species. External situations change and in general increase in number and variety. The additions made by the telescope and microscope and telephone and radio are the most obvious evidence of this, but the change from no huts, no clothing, no tools, and no domestic animals to even a few meant a substantial and notable enrichment of the stimuli to man's mind. The change from a few instinctive cries, chuckles, and cooings to even the simplest articulate language, say, one with names for only fifty feelings, things, or events, was a similar enrichment, with far-reaching promise.

The repertory of overt responses changes and increases not much perhaps in its elementary movements, since the instinctive gurglings, prattlings, wrigglings, thrustings, wavings, etc. of infancy may include most of these, but greatly in their combinations. The words of speech are of course, the most striking case. The movements made in using clubs, knives, hammers, hoes, cups, and other tools and implements make another great group.

New elements become active in determining response and in forming preferential bonds. Instead of edibility, obstructiveness, reachableness, fitness for a club, and other such, we have roundness, squareness, sharpness, twoness, threeness, and so on to velocity, acceleration, voltage, amperage, and specific gravity.

Some of the new situations and responses are powerful tools for further learning. A shorthand symbolism for real things, events, and relations develops, first in ordinary language and later in the special technical languages of arithmetic, algebra, physics, chemistry, and the other sciences. Thinking has been so much aided by language that there has been much debate whether it could exist without language. Certainly, human learning could not get far or go fast without some such symbols. The use of waste air from the lungs to make sounds which attract, frighten, warn, encourage, and the like is one of the most interesting variations in the animal kingdom. Its development into articulate speech is perhaps man's greatest invention or series of inventions. At slight expense of energy, with a minimum of interference with bodily action in general, with a repertory of a score or two of responses, forming by combination thousands of identifiable syllables, and millions of identifiable two-syllable words, producible at the rate of a hundred per minute, man can influence hearers at all points within a wide radius.

A conservative estimate of the amount that the average person in a civilized country learns via words * plus direct experience of things, events, qualities, and relations compared to what he could learn by the latter alone would be

* Or some artificial translation of them, as in the sign manual of the deaf and dumb.

well over ten to one. It is partly by hearing an object named that the infant learns to identify it in spite of different views of it from different distances and in different contexts. It is largely by preferential bonds with their names that the qualities and aspects and relations of things and events are analyzed out into relief. By the connection of a word with this, that, and the other object or event, we form our first concepts. By the connection of a word with such and such a combination of facts or qualities or features, we refine them and add to them. It is no wonder that man used to think that words had magical power, and that if you could call any object or force of nature by the appropriate name you would have power over it. Indeed we do. By calling diphtheria the Klebs-Loeffler bacillus we do gain power over it, though not in the vague and general way of magic.

A system of numbers is a part of language so power-ful as a tool for thought and action that it is usually treated by itself. A child who grows up hearing collections of objects called two, three, ten, twenty, a hundred, a million, and hearing lengths, weights, and times called three feet, thirty pounds, five minutes, and the like, learns to think of things as countable and measurable almost as he learns to wear clothes or blow his nose. He expects everything to have a name, and he expects many things to be definable in amounts. As he goes to school and to work, he enters a world of systematic measurement and computation. Numbers are tools that enable him to understand and manage it.

At a more advanced level we have such tools as the equa-tion or formula, which enable men to learn in a few hours fundamental and pervasive features of the behavior of things which he could otherwise learn only imperfectly with great labor or not at all.

The host of physical tools to aid learning I may barely mention. We have boats and trains and airplanes to transport us to countless situations, cameras, telephones, and radios to bring all sorts of stimuli to us, clocks, thermometers, scales, compasses, galvanometers, and the like to define stimuli exactly, alphabets to record speech, pens and typewriters and printing presses to make and multiply the records, and books to preserve them.

As has already been suggested, these tools, psychological and physical, make situations and elements of situations more easily and more exactly identifiable. The ablest judge of distance of 100,000 years ago could not have measured the height of a tree as accurately as a school-boy can now. At that time there probably was no man living who could tell 100 sheep from 101.

They also make available responses which were once far beyond man's grasp. With a yardstick a fool can draw a straight line thirty inches long more accurately than the best artist and judge of length can without it.

We do not have to go back anywhere near 100,000 years to reach a time when a man could have gained great repute as a wizard if on seeing 100 coconuts and fifteen persons, he could predict that there would be six per person and ten left over. If some man of a few thousand years ago had wished to draw a square or a circle to contain ten square units, he could not have done so.

Man to-day can make connections ending in responses of generating 1,000,000 volts of electricity or letting loose a pestilence, tasks for only Jove and Apollo not long ago.

The situations which men face have multiplied; elements or parts or aspects of them which are distinguished have multiplied; the responses which men have available for use have multiplied. So a child of to-day forms scores or even hundreds of connections where the child of 1,000 generations ago formed one. The average American child of fourteen, for example, knows more or less well the meanings of 10,000 words.

Even more important than this increase in the quantity of learning are the changes in its quality. Notions about fairies and demons are replaced by notions about oxygen and hydrogen and volts and amperes and radio frequencies. Fears of witches and devils give way to fears of typhoid and tuberculosis. Much of learning has been learning that certain opinions once cherished are not true or useful. The universe of early man, small as it was, consisted in large measure of false gods, imaginary forces, events that had not occurred, and illusory hopes and fears.

How and why man has burdened his mind with so great a load of fantastic errors and superstitions is an interesting problem. Why has he gone out of his way to invent charms, fetishes, and idols instead of better clubs and arrows? Why has he peopled the world with demons to plague him and wasted his substance in sacrifices to them? Why should there have been such a multitudinous and incessant production of mental variations toward error and folly? And why, when they were produced, did they not die childless?

If mind and thought are, as the philosophers used to assert, powers designed to seek and recognize the truth, these questions are unanswerable. But apparently nature's gift to man is not a sense of truth versus error, but only an ability to connect and keep together what ideas have gone together and to favor those connections which are immediately satisfying, plus, as we have seen, an organization of neurones and muscles which make possible an enormous number of complex and delicate and piecemeal connections, giving a rich life of ideas.

The ability to have such ideas at all has apparently been so useful in enabling man to survive that he could suffer innumerable fantasies and perversions along with it. Putting the seed in the soil at spring-tide and offering therewith a sacrifice to Ceres is on the whole a profitable venture, even though part of it is wasteful. The ability to make fire with sticks and incantations is valuable enough to support not only those incantations, but hundreds of others of no value at all.

So man has learned in past ages an extraordinary mixture of truth and error, of things pertinent and irrelevant to a successful life. All sorts of connections are made by the minds of men—that this stone which I picked up just before killing a deer will bring good fortune in the chase, that drinking the blood of a lion will make you brave, that night air gives people malaria, that not night air but mosquitoes give it to them, that three is a favorable number, that a number to mean not any or none at all will be useful, that the sun is a man, and the moon a woman, that the world does not treat me as well as I deserve, that we should not eat pork, that we should eat vitamines, that women should obey their husbands, that women should be allowed to vote, that we may well indicate roots by fractional exponents, etc., etc.

Some of these connections are made public by their authors. Some are not. Of those made public, some are acceptable to a large fraction of the community and are perpetuated in beliefs and customs.

Within recent times science and scholarship have worked over this mass of intermingled truth and error, wisdom and folly, separating the true from the false and adding enormously to the true that men may learn if they will. The methods of science are impartial, paying no heed to the immediate satisfyingness of any idea to any individual. They require verification and test by prophecy. They produce thinkers whose minds are, with respect to the special problems involved, repositories of facts—systems of connections all tried and true—and so well fitted to have fruitful ideas.

The results of science have been almost universally acceptable to the community in the fields of physics, chemistry, and the other physical sciences, somewhat less so in the biological sciences, and still less so in the psychological and social sciences. On the whole, we may take pride in the probability that the human beings born this year will learn a very much greater amount of truth and a somewhat higher percentage of truth than any previous generation.

The evolution of learning has been toward learning more things and truer things, and also (at least recently) toward learning equally difficult things more quickly and pleasantly. The last fact is obscured to observation by the much wider, and so inferior, selection of learners now than fifty years ago. And my assertion of it is based on circumstantial rather than direct evidence. I am sure, however, that competent and impartial observation of schools of the present in comparison with those of the past would confirm it. The methods of the past we may also fairly safely infer from its instruments of instruction. I quote two samples from an arithmetic of our grandparents and from the famous Spelling Book of Noah Webster.

LESSON I

1. In this picture, how many girls are in the swing?
2. How many girls are pulling the swing?
3. If you count both girls together, how many are they? *One* girl and *one* other girl are how many?
4. How many kittens do you see on the stump?
5. How many on the ground?
6. How many kittens are in the picture? One kitten and one other kitten are how many?
7. If you should ask me how many girls are in the swing, or how many kittens are on the stump, I could answer aloud, "One"; or I could write *One;* or thus, *1.*
8. If I write *One,* this is called the *word One.*
9. This, *1,* is named a *figure One,* because it means the same as the word *One,* and stands for *One.*
10. Write 1. What is this named? Why?
11. A figure 1 may stand for *one* girl, *one* kitten, or *one* anything.
12. When children first attend school, what do they begin to learn? *Ans.* Letters and words.
13. Could you read or write before you had learned either letters or words?
14. If we have all the *letters* together, they are named the Alphabet.
15. If we write or speak *words,* they are named Language.
16. You are commencing to study Arithmetic; and you can read and write in Arithmetic only as you learn the Alphabet and Language of Arithmetic. But little time will be required for this purpose.

LESSON II

1. If we speak or write words, what do we name them, when taken together?
2. What are you commencing to study? *Ans.* Arithmetic.
3. What Language must you now learn?
4. What do we name this, 1? Why?
5. This figure, 1, is part of the Language of Arithmetic.
6. If I should write something to stand for Two—*two* girls, *two* kittens, or *two* things of any kind—what do you think we would name it?
7. A *figure Two* is written thus: 2. Make a *figure two.*
8. Why do we name this a *figure two?*
9. This figure two (2) is part of the Language of Arithmetic.
10. In this picture one boy is sitting, playing a flageolet. What is the other boy doing? If the boy standing should sit down by the other, how many boys would be sitting together? One boy and one other boy are how many boys?
11. You see a flageolet and a violin. They are musical instruments. One musical instrument and one other musical instrument are how many?
12. I will write thus: $1 + 1 = 2$. We say that 1 boy and 1 other boy, counted together, are 2 boys; or are equal to 2 boys. We will now write something to show that the first 1 and the other 1 are to be counted together.
13. We name a line drawn thus, —, a *horizontal line.* Draw such a line. Name it.
14. A line drawn thus, |, we name a *vertical line.* Draw such a line. Name it.
15. Now I will put two such lines together; thus, +. What kind of a line do we name the first (—)? And what do we name the last? (|)? Are these lines long or short? Where do they cross each other?
16. Each of you write thus: —, |, +.
17. This, +, is named Plus. *Plus* means *more;* and + also means *more.*
18. I will write
    One and One More Equal Two.
    $$1 + 1 = 2$$

ba	be	bi	bo	bu	by
ca	ce	ci	co	cu	cy
da	de	di	do	du	dy
fa	fe	fi	fo	fu	fy
ka	ke	ki	ko	ku	ky

ga	ge	gi	go	gu	gy
ha	he	hi	ho	hu	hy
ma	me	mi	mo	mu	my
na	ne	ni	no	nu	ny
ra	re	ri	ro	ru	ry
ta	te	ti	to	tu	ty
wa	we	wi	wo	wu	wy

la	le	li	lo	lu	ly
pa	pe	pi	po	pu	py
sa	se	si	so	su	sy
za	ze	zi	zo	zu	zy

ab	eb	ib	ob	ub
ac	ec	ic	oc	uc
ad	ed	id	od	ud
af	ef	if	of	uf
al	el	il	ol	ul

ag	eg	ig	og	ug
am	em	im	om	um
an	en	in	on	un
ap	ep	ip	op	up
as	es	is	os	us
av	ev	iv	ov	uv
ax	ex	ix	ox	ux

ak	ek	ik	ok	uk
at	et	it	ot	ut
ar	er	ir	or	ur
az	ez	iz	oz	uz

bla	ble	bli	blo	blu	
cla	cle	cli	clo	clu	
pla	ple	pli	plo	plu	
fla	fle	fli	flo	flu	
va	ve	vi	vo	vu	

bra	bre	bri	bro	bru	
cra	cre	cri	cro	cru	
pra	pre	pri	pro	pru	
gra	gre	gri	gro	gru	
pha	phe	phi	pho	phu	

cha	che	chi	cho	chu	chy
dra	dre	dri	dro	dru	dry
fra	fre	fri	fro	fru	fry
gla	gle	gli	glo	glu	gly

sla	sle	sli	slo	slu	sly
qua	que	qui	quo		
sha	she	shi	sho	shu	shy
spa	spe	spi	spo	spu	spy

sta	ste	sti	sto	stu	sty
sca	sce	sci	sco	scu	scy
tha	the	thi	tho	thu	thy
tra	tre	tri	tro	tru	try

spla	sple	spli	splo	splu	sply
spra	spre	spri	spro	spru	spry
stra	stre	stri	stro	stru	stry
swa	swe	swi	swo	swu	swy

The future evolution of intellect and learning has been forecast by romancers, but never, I think, by psychologists. I am tempted to abandon their prudent reticence in the few minutes that remain, and picture the learners and learning of 1,000 or 10,000 years hence. But it will be safer and on the whole more instructive to state only probabilities and possibilities in general terms.

Probably man will learn more; more of what he learns will be true and wise; he will learn it more quickly and comfortably. The distribution of learning among the population will be better organized.

I need not enlarge upon any of these prophecies save the last. At present, the distribution of learning by schools is largely indiscriminate, the active ideal being to have as many children as possible learn as much as possible, with very little regard to who learns what. The distribution of learning in after life is due to individual choice under the guidance partly of benevolent institutions such as homes, churches, libraries, or settlements, and partly (and increasingly) under the guidance of commercial concerns working for profits. The benevolent forces work in too great disregard of what people really want; the commercial concerns are under the constant temptation to stimulate the baser wants.

So there is now considerable danger that many individuals will learn much that they cannot either enjoy or use for the common good, and that some individuals will fail to learn what they need to make them happy and useful. The scientific study of human nature by the idealists and reformers and the development of finer standards of success in business will, it may be hoped and believed, produce a much better distribution of learning.

Of what sort the learners of the future will be, we do not know, but of the possibility of eugenics in intellect and character there can be no doubt. Human individuals differ by original nature as cats and dogs and tulips and roses do. They differ as truly and probably as much in the genes which determine intellect and character as in the genes which determine height or strength or facial appearance. Intellect is apparently the result not of one or two determiners but of many, so that the task of breeding high ability in or breeding idiocy out is much more complicated and laborious than the task of getting or getting rid of curliness of hair or pinkness of blossom. But it is not impossible. I dare to believe that a time may come when a child born an idiot by germinal defect will be as rare as a child with twelve toes.

The danger that selection for intellect will involve deterioration in health or mental balance or morals or anything else is non-existent, or easily avoidable. As a rule, breeding better intellects will mean breeding men better in other respects as well. The danger of deterioration in social conditions as a result of breeding for intellect or character is trivial. The effect is much more likely to be a betterment. The more intelligent the race becomes, the better environment it will construct for itself. The more its genes favor wisdom and justice, the better customs and laws it will create.

How intelligent it may become is uncertain. But if mankind really wanted to improve the nature of its children as much as it wants to improve the conditions of life for itself and them, it could certainly hope within 100 generations to have a race of men whose average would be much nearer to the intellect of Newton, Pasteur, Gladstone, and Edison than to that of the average man of to-day. Its upper limit may or may not be set by conditions beyond human control, but its average may be moved toward that upper limit by even the simplest and crudest types of selective breeding.

We have much to learn about eugenics, but even now we know enough to urge us to provide the intellect of man with higher and purer sources than the muddy streams of the past. If it is our duty to improve the quality of what is learned and the means of learning it, it is doubly our duty to improve the original inborn ability of man to learn. There is no surer way of improving civilization than by improving man's own nature.

Ethics and religion must teach man to want the welfare of the future as well as the relief of the cripple before his eyes; and science must teach man to control his own future nature as well as the animals, plants, and physical forces amongst which he will have to live. It is a noble thing that human reason, bred of a myriad unreasoned happenings, and driven forth into life by whips made æons ago with no thought of man's higher wants, can yet turn back to understand man's birth, survey his journey, chart and steer his future course, and free him from barriers without and defects within. Until the last removable impediment in man's own nature dies childless, human reason will not rest.

BIBLIOGRAPHY OF REFERENCES IN THE TEXT

Brown, H. W.   '92 Some records of the thoughts and reasonings of children. *Pedagogical Seminary*, Vol. 2, pp. 358-396.

James, W.   '93 *Principles of Psychology.*

Koffka, K.   '25 *The Growth of the Mind.*

Köhler, W.   '25 *The Mentality of Apes.*

Ogden, R. M.   '26 *Psychology and Education.*

Pavlov, I. P.   '27 *Conditioned Reflexes.*

Piéron, H.   '11a Sur la détermination de la période d'établissement dans les acquisitions mnémoniques. *Comptes rendus Acad. Sci.*, Vol. 152, p. 1410.

           '11b Les courbes d'évanouissement des traces mnémoniques. *Comptes rendus Acad. Sci.*, Vol. 152, p. 1115.

Symanski, J. S.   '12 Modification of the innate behavior of cockroaches. *Journal of Animal Behavior*, Vol. 2, pp. 81-90.

Thorndike, E. L.   '98 Animal Intelligence. *Psychological Review*, Monograph Supplement No. 8.

           '01 The mental life of the monkeys. *Psychological Review*, Monograph Supplement No. 15.

Tilton, J. W.   '26 The relation between association and the higher mental processes. *Teachers College, Columbia University, Contributions to Education* (No. 218).

Turner, C. H.   '12   An experimental investigation of an apparent reversal of the light responses of the roach (*Periplaneta Orientalis L.*). *Biological Bulletin,* Vol. 23, pp. 371-386.

Warden, C. J., and Aylesworth, M.   '27   The relative value of reward and punishment in the formation of a visual discrimination habit in the white rat. *Journal of Comparative Psychology,* 1927, 7, pp. 117-128.

Yerkes, R. M.   '02   Habit formation in the green crab *Carcinus granulatus*. *Biological Bulletin,* Vol. 3, pp. 241-244.

     '12   The intelligence of earthworms. *Journal of Animal Behavior,* Vol. 2, pp. 332-352.

Yerkes, R. M., and Huggins, G. E.   '03   Habit formation in the crawfish, *cambarus affinis*. *Psychological Review,* Monograph Supplement No. 17, pp. 565-577.

INDEX

THE M.I.T. PAPERBACK SERIES